Emily Carr

SERIES EDITOR:
John Ralston Saul

Emily Carr

by LEWIS DeSOTO

With an Introduction by
John Ralston Saul
SERIES EDITOR

PENGUIN CANADA

Published by the Penguin Group

Penguin Group (Canada), 90 Eglinton Avenue East, Suite 700, Toronto, Ontario, Canada
M4P 2Y3 (a division of Pearson Canada Inc.)

Penguin Group (USA) Inc., 375 Hudson Street, New York, New York 10014, U.S.A.
Penguin Books Ltd, 80 Strand, London WC2R 0RL, England
Penguin Ireland, 25 St Stephen's Green, Dublin 2, Ireland
(a division of Penguin Books Ltd)
Penguin Group (Australia), 250 Camberwell Road, Camberwell, Victoria 3124, Australia
(a division of Pearson Australia Group Pty Ltd)
Penguin Books India Pvt Ltd, 11 Community Centre, Panchsheel Park,
New Delhi – 110 017, India
Penguin Group (NZ), 67 Apollo Drive, Rosedale, North Shore 0745, Auckland,
New Zealand (a division of Pearson New Zealand Ltd)
Penguin Books (South Africa) (Pty) Ltd, 24 Sturdee Avenue, Rosebank,
Johannesburg 2196, South Africa

Penguin Books Ltd, Registered Offices: 80 Strand, London WC2R 0RL, England

First published 2008

1 2 3 4 5 6 7 8 9 10 (RRD)

Copyright © Lewis DeSoto, 2008
Introduction copyright © John Ralston Saul, 2008

Manufactured in the U.S.A.

ISBN-13: 978-0-670-06670-4
ISBN-10: 0-670-06670-2

Library and Archives Canada Cataloguing in Publication
data available upon request.

Visit the Penguin Group (Canada) website at **www.penguin.ca**

Special and corporate bulk purchase rates available; please see **www.penguin.ca/
corporatesales** or call 1-800-810-3104, ext. 477 or 474

This book was printed on 30% PCW recycled paper

CONTENTS

John Ralston Saul

How do civilizations imagine themselves? One way is for each of us to look at ourselves through our society's most remarkable figures. I'm not talking about hero worship or political iconography. That is a danger to be avoided at all costs. And yet people in every country do keep on going back to the most important people in their past.

This series of Extraordinary Canadians brings together rebels, reformers, martyrs, writers, painters, thinkers, political leaders. Why? What is it that makes them relevant to us so long after their deaths?

For one thing, their contributions are there before us, like the building blocks of our society. More important than that are their convictions and drive, their sense of what is right and wrong, their willingness to risk all, whether it be their lives, their reputations, or simply being wrong in public. Their ideas, their triumphs and failures, all of these somehow constitute a mirror of our society. We look at these people, all dead, and discover what we have been, but also what we can be. A mirror is an instrument for measuring ourselves. What we see can be both a warning and an encouragement.

These eighteen biographies of twenty key Canadians are centred on the meaning of each of their lives. Each of them is very different, but these are not randomly chosen great figures. Together they produce a grand sweep of the creation of modern Canada, from our first steps as a democracy in 1848 to our questioning of modernity late in the twentieth century.

All of them except one were highly visible on the cutting edge of their day while still in their twenties, thirties, and forties. They were young, driven, curious. An astonishing level of fresh energy surrounded them and still does. We in the twenty-first century talk endlessly of youth, but power today is often controlled by people who fear the sort of risks and innovations embraced by everyone in this series. A number of them were dead—hanged, infected on a battlefield, broken by their exertions—well before middle age. Others hung on into old age, often profoundly dissatisfied with themselves.

Each one of these people has changed you. In some cases you know this already. In others you will discover how through these portraits. They changed the way the world hears music, thinks of war, communicates. They changed how each of us sees what surrounds us, how minorities are treated, how we think of immigrants, how we look after each other, how we imagine ourselves through what are now our stories.

You will notice that many of them were people of the word. Not just the writers. Why? Because civilizations are built around many themes, but they require a shared public language. So Laurier, Bethune, Douglas, Riel, LaFontaine, McClung, Trudeau, Lévesque, Big Bear, even Carr and Gould, were masters of the power of language. Beaverbrook was one of the most powerful newspaper publishers of his day. Countries need action and laws and courage. But civilization is not a collection of prime ministers. Words, words, words—it is around these that civilizations create and imagine themselves.

The authors I have chosen for each subject are not the obvious experts. They are imaginative, questioning minds from among our leading writers and activists. They have, each one of them, a powerful connection to their subject. And in their own lives, each is engaged in building what Canada is now becoming.

That is why a documentary is being filmed around each subject. Images are yet another way to get at each subject and to understand their effect on us.

There has not been a biographical project as ambitious as this in a hundred years, not since the Makers of Canada series. And yet every generation understands the past differently, and so sees in the mirror of these remarkable figures somewhat different lessons.

What strikes me again and again is just how dramatically ethical decisions figured in their lives. They form the backbone of history and memory. Some of these people, Big Bear, for example, or Dumont, or even Lucy Maud Montgomery, thought of themselves as failures by the end of their lives. But the ethical cord that was strung taut through their work has now carried them on to a new meaning and even greater strength, long after their deaths.

Each of these stories is a revelation of the tough choices unusual people must make to find their way. And each of us as readers will find in the desperation of the Chinese revolution, the search for truth in fiction, the political and military dramas, different meanings that strike a personal chord. At first it is that personal emotive link to such figures which draws us in. Then we find they are a key that opens the whole society of their time to us. Then we realize that in that 150-year period many of them knew each other, were friends, opposed each other. Finally, when all these stories are put together, you will see that a whole new debate has been created around Canadian civilization and the shape of our continuous experiment.

Emily Carr is like an iron rod running through this whole debate. I had always felt there was something deeply rigorous and original in her paintings. Here Lewis DeSoto has found a way to the heart of her toughness. Art historians like to talk about how painters were influenced by others. Many Canadian art historians prefer to see our painters as not just influenced by, but derivative of, European schools. Certainly Carr picked up things here and there. Every painter everywhere does that. But what is remarkable is just how original Carr is. Along with Paul-Émile Borduas, she is our greatest painter. She somehow summoned up the deep heart not just of the British Columbia forest, but of Canada as forest and Canada as Aboriginal. That's why people all over the country so instinctively identify with her images. This mysterious place is us. Emily Carr, with her toughness and humour and writing skills, is a sharp reminder of how edgy Canadians need to be to occupy this enormous, difficult space.

Emily Carr

CHAPTER ONE

A Meeting

I didn't like Emily Carr. The paintings, that is. I knew nothing of the woman herself. I first encountered her work when I was studying painting in Vancouver at what would later be renamed the Emily Carr College of Art and Design, housed in a building within sight of the spot where she once had a studio.

When I used to visit the Vancouver Art Gallery, it seemed as though most of the rooms were given over to Carr's paintings—dark and brooding pictures of forests and totem poles. What I wanted to see instead was the new, bright, contemporary art that was being made in New York and London, not paintings made a hundred years ago by some little old lady who lived in the woods.

Some years later, a painter myself and interested in the landscape, I paid a visit to my father on Saturna Island, an hour's boat ride from Victoria. One afternoon, I took what I thought was a shortcut back from the cove and somehow missed a fork in the path. Within minutes I found myself standing alone in the deep forest that covers most of the island.

The silence was absolute, almost a palpable physical presence. The tall, rust-coloured tree trunks of fir and cedar soared upward like the pillars of an ancient temple, and the shafts of sunlight falling down through the canopy glowed like molten gold. The swooping boughs of foliage seemed to hang in frozen waves of green—such a variety of greens.

A raven croaked overhead, with that deep hollow sound they sometimes make, and in the following silence I heard its wings like a whisper in the trees.

I sensed the vastness of this country, the emptiness of it, all the ancient days of it. I felt as if I were standing in a place where no human had stood, and none might ever stand again. I was nothing, an insignificant passing sigh on the breeze. A moment of unaccountable terror shivered over me.

An image of an Emily Carr painting came to my mind, of a forest like this one, with the same primeval grandeur. But in that painting, the dread and solitude had been subsumed into a reverent harmony, as if the silence and the awe, the leaves and the raven, and the lone human being were part of a grand creation that could be approached only with wonder and celebration. I realized how much the scene in front of me looked like an Emily Carr painting. It was almost as if I were seeing it through her eyes. Those paintings that I used to frown at and dismiss had somehow imprinted themselves on my consciousness, in such a powerful manner that what I saw before me now was less a forest of trees and leaves and more a work of art, half nature, half Emily Carr.

Later, I went back to the art gallery and looked again at the paintings. I began to be interested in this woman, whom I really knew nothing about. Who was she? Where did she come from? How had she lived? And, above all, how had she arrived at her extraordinary paintings?

I would encounter a truly remarkable and talented woman who lived with bravado and curiosity. Not only was she physically brave and strong, but she also possessed deep psychological courage. She was not some little old lady in the woods, but a complex and contradictory individual who lived a noteworthy and varied existence of great originality, and in so doing made a part of the world visible in all its beauty and mystery.

The tourist who visits the museums, the hiker in the rain-forest, the visitor who buys a postcard of a Carr painting because it seems to contain some essence of this part of the country, the new immigrant turning the pages of a history of Canada, even the descendants of the original inhabitants of the West Coast—all see this place with just a little bit of Emily Carr in their vision.

Emily Carr, the person, defies easy description. Painter, writer, world traveller, adventurer—she was also an original, a rebel, a free spirit, and a visionary mystic. She is one of those unique individuals, those few, who have created and articulated the symbols and images by which Canada knows itself, and through which we know ourselves.

CHAPTER TWO

The Past

Writing about the past is like standing on a cliff edge looking into the mist while trying to recognize a person you have never met. There is no truth about the past—there are versions only. But that does not preclude our attempts to know it. Curiosity is justification enough. In a time that is remote from us now, Emily Carr stands as an icon, a colossus almost, and if only for that reason she draws our attention.

The elements in society that make reputations, that drive the buying and selling of art, that publicize and celebrate and define art, are not found in provincial cities but in the great urban centres of the world. Emily chose to remain in her small corner. If she had lived in Paris, London, or Berlin, or if the technology of communication and travel that exists now had been available in her time, then every book on the history of art would include an Emily Carr. Her works would hang in the Tate Modern in London, the Louvre in Paris, and the Metropolitan Museum of Art in New York. That is where they belong, alongside Vincent van Gogh and Edvard Munch and Paul Cézanne.

Nevertheless, Emily's name is in our history books. A busy industry revolves around Emily Carr: academics write and argue about her; museums mount exhibitions of her work; the tourist business markets her life and images; her childhood house is a museum. Her story, with its drama and eccentricity, satisfies our need for larger-than-life figures with whom to populate our mythology. Her paintings are reproduced on postage stamps, calendars, and postcards. Novels have been written about her, films made, even a stage play. Along with the Group of Seven and Tom Thomson, she is, for many, the best-known Canadian artist. But more than that, her work is among the images of Canada itself.

We see the West Coast landscape through the prism of Emily Carr's paintings, just as much as the central Ontario landscape is filtered through the paintings of the Group of Seven. There are no paintings that describe the coastal rainforest before Emily. That is the mark of her originality—not her technique or colours or style. She gave a form and a meaning to a landscape. Her paintings are images through which Canada becomes visible, to us and to others.

In the end, the paintings are what remain—the most significant verifiable fact in the history of Emily Carr. We need to know nothing of the artist, her times, or the context in which the paintings were made to respond to them as art. But an image is never either neutral or mute. We can say with certainty of the paintings only that they are made of canvas and pigment. What they say to us depends as much on what we know as on what we don't know. And so we must try to know the woman, if only to consider what other things the paintings speak of. As she put it in her journal, "Something of you can get trapped forever in the picture as long as it lasts." Each one of her paintings is the evidence of a woman's hand. Each brush stroke is the trace of a gesture and a thought.

For all the words written by and about Emily Carr, she remains something of an enigma. We continue to be fascinated by her, this woman who travelled to the wild, dark places and returned to tell us the tale of where she had been.

WE CAN NEVER REALLY KNOW anyone from the past. There are some facts, some speculations, many opinions, and a great many disagreements. There are Emily Carr's writings, her correspondence, some photos. And, of course, there are the paintings. In the end, there is only an interpretation, and the hope of a small measure of truth.

The past does leave a legacy that accumulates, and through which we can understand ourselves. Emily Carr is situated in our history now, and the legacy she left, in her paintings and writings and in the trajectory of her life, is a part of that always-forming idea we call Canada.

A common error we make when thinking about distant times is to imagine them as somehow old-fashioned, and the people who inhabited another era to be equally out of date. We look backward into time and see its inhabitants as being ignorant, quaint, and mistaken in so much. But every person is always born into a modern world, every moment is the lived present, on the threshold of the future.

The ancient Romans did not think of themselves as ancient; the Haida fisherman on the Queen Charlotte Islands knew his world to be new each time the sun rose; the child walking to school in 1881 did not think it was quaint to live in the Victorian age. All of them lived in the present, in what was for them the most modern era yet, in the most advanced of times.

When we look at photographs of Emily Carr and the world she lived in, we are apt to smile condescendingly at the rather comical fashions: the silly hats and uncomfortable dresses, the tightly buttoned gentlemen in their top hats, the horse-drawn buggies and paddle steamers. But it was all modern in its day.

The same can be said of the art of the past. The bright colours of Monet and Van Gogh and the daring geometry of early abstraction are part of the history of art now. We are accustomed to them. But in their time they all had the shocking strangeness of the new. So, too, with the paintings of Emily Carr. No matter how much a part of our world they are now, each one as it appeared on her canvas was something the world had not seen before.

Today we embrace originality in art and in life. If Emily had been born into our time, with her talent, her independence, and her ambition, she almost certainly would have been famous at a young age rather than remaining an unknown artist for most of her life. The Emily Carrs of today have cell phones and computers. Some of them become celebrities who represent Canada in international exhibitions like the Venice Biennale, give interviews to glossy magazines, command high prices for their work, set trends, and define styles. That they are able to do so, women as well as men, in a way that Emily Carr never dreamed of is due in no small part to the example of her courage and determination to be an artist.

CHAPTER THREE

Victoria

So, let us take a walk with Emily, back and forth through time, starting outside the Carr house in the neighbourhood of James Bay, a quiet residential area on the southern side of Victoria's Inner Harbour, a short stroll from the city centre.

The house is now a museum, on a small plot on Government Street, which used to be known as Carr Street, and before that, when the house was first built on its eight acres of land, was just a grassy country lane. Woods stood here, flower and vegetable gardens, an orchard, a barn for cows and pigs. To the left as we go down the street is Beacon Hill Park, now mostly landscaped but still wild and uncultivated in parts, as it was when the young Emily wandered here.

After a couple of blocks, we reach the Pacific Ocean. A marker on the shoreline denotes Mile Zero of the Trans-Canada Highway. Some say that Canada begins here, others that it ends at this spot.

Most maps of Canada terminate at this point, but just across the Strait of Juan de Fuca are the Olympic Mountains of Washington State and a coastline that extends to San Francisco and beyond. Travel west across the Pacific Ocean and the first landfall will be Japan. To the east, across another body of water (the Strait of Georgia), reminding us that Victoria is on an island, lies Vancouver and the vast mainland of Canada. A journey north up the coast will take you to the Queen Charlotte Islands—or to give them their original name, Haida Gwaii—and onward to Alaska.

On her walk in the 1880s, Emily might have seen some Native canoes pulled up at a campsite on the shore, beached there by people coming from up the coast to either trade or visit. Today we see a line of buses waiting at the dock for the giant cruise ships that bring tourists to Victoria in their thousands each summer. A Coast Guard station sits at the entrance to the harbour now. The float planes that make the trip to Vancouver in a half-hour buzz overhead and then skim into James Bay. A trip across to Vancouver would have taken Emily a full day.

At Laurel Point, where the shoreline turns into the harbour proper, a meandering walkway lined with flowerbeds passes in front of the deluxe hotels. We can look across the bay to Songhees Point, where tall, luxurious condominiums have spread along the shore. The Songhees First Nation used to live there, part of the Salishan people, and in

Emily's youth the Songhees reserve had some two thousand inhabitants.

Our walk brings us to the provincial parliament buildings, which were completed in 1896, just a year after Queen Victoria's Diamond Jubilee. At the terminus of the harbour stands the Empress Hotel, another reminder that this was, after all, an outpost of the British Empire.

In the days of Emily's youth, Victoria was still something of a frontier town. The sidewalks were wooden and transportation was by horse and coach. But the city was growing rapidly. There were many new buildings of stone and brick, including warehouses, churches, and hotels. Today it has a university, an art gallery, a symphony orchestra, and is Canada's fifteenth-largest city.

Near the legislature stands the Royal B.C. Museum and Thunderbird Park, which contains a Native longhouse and a number of totem poles. This is probably Victoria's most popular stop for tourists. If Emily could see the park today, she might view it with some irony. She once offered a collection of her paintings to the museum, but the proposal was rejected. In the years after Emily's death her paintings would be exhibited here many times, but at the time of her passing only one of her works was in the provincial collection.

Emily's path would have brought her now to a bridge leading into the city proper, where the little girl used to walk hand in hand with her father each morning, and meet him again at the end of the day when he returned from his place of business.

The Carr family was a respectable, Victorian colonial household of comfortable means. The parents were English born, and had lived for some years in California before settling in Victoria. Emily was the youngest of five girls. Her brother, Dick, the last child, was four years younger. When Emily was born her father was fifty-three and her mother thirty-five. There was a difference of fifteen years between Emily and her eldest sister, Edith. Emily was called Milly, to distinguish her from her mother, who had the same name. Sometimes she was also called Small, a name she would resurrect when she wrote about her childhood in *The Book of Small* many years later.

Richard Carr left his home in England as a young man and travelled in Europe and then on the American continent, from Peru to northern Canada, working at a variety of occupations. He saw much of the rough side of life, but always retained his British manner and ideals. He made his money as a merchant in California and then in Victoria, with a warehouse on Wharf Street within walking distance of the house he built in James Bay.

Little is known about Emily's mother. She met Richard Carr in California and returned to England to marry him there, where they lived for five years. But as his daughter was to do later, Richard Carr chafed at the confines of English society, disliked the dreary weather, and longed for the openness of North America. The Carrs settled in Victoria. Like their fellow citizens, finding themselves positioned between the unruly United States and the wild North, they clung to their British heritage. They became in many respects more English than the English themselves.

Childhood was a happy time for Emily. She was adventuresome and lively. She was very fond of animals and spent as much time outdoors as she could. Her usual companions were her sisters Lizzie and Alice, who were closest to her in age. The two older girls, Edith and Clara, were practically adults. The youngest child, Dick, was sickly, and was kept close to his mother.

As the youngest girl Emily was indulged and pampered. She was the favourite of her father, but that ended when she entered her teenage years, when father and daughter became estranged from each other. For the remaining years of Richard Carr's life a distance existed between them, laying the foundation for Emily's always unresolved relations with men in later life.

Under Richard Carr's guidance, the household was pious, and religion played an important part in their routine. They said prayers each weekday morning and attendance at church on Sundays was obligatory. Sunday was not for leisure or picnics, but was filled with hymn singing, Bible readings, and Sunday school for the children. Emily would always have deep spiritual yearnings that would be an important element in her art and life, but they would not be satisfied in orthodox Christianity.

We are all shaped by our beginnings. However much we strive to make our own way, the circumstances of early life are the markers setting the course of our life's journey. For Emily, childhood ended when her mother died at the age of fifty, probably from tuberculosis. Emily was fifteen years old. Two years later her father also died. Edith, the eldest sister, aged thirty-two, became the head of the family. Edith had always occupied a position of authority and there had been strife between her and Emily, who, despite being shy, was already something of a rebel. She possessed a restless and independent spirit quite different from that of her sisters.

The Carrs were suddenly a household of four women on their own with one small sickly boy. The house was willed to Edith and the finances of the family were entrusted to a guardian. Clara had left home and married six years earlier. (She would be the only one of the Carr sisters to do so, and would later divorce.) Lizzie was studying to be a missionary, and Alice to be a schoolteacher. Emily had finished elementary school, but had completed only one year of high school.

A photograph of Emily in 1890, aged eighteen, shows a pretty young woman with long curly hair, intelligent eyes in a round face, arched eyebrows, and a shy smile. An interest in drawing had manifested itself in Emily over the years, and had been encouraged with lessons. Her declared aim in life was to be an artist. As her father had been something of a traveller before settling down, she may have inherited his wanderlust. In any event, she decided to escape what was now an oppressive and broken household and go to San Francisco to study art.

It would be the first of numerous departures and returns. Victoria's location, on the edge between the old British society and the new Canada, would have a profound effect on Emily Carr, remaining a source of pride and conflict, becoming both the cause of her failure and the reason for her success.

More than the city, it was the landscape that would call to her—the forests, the mountains, and the sea. Always they would call to her, wherever she was. In their mystery and their wildness she would find herself, she would find her art, and she would find something of Canada itself. Later, she put it this way in her journal *Hundreds and Thousands:*

> I am always asking myself the question, What is it that you are struggling for? What is the vital thing the woods contain, possess, that you want? Why do you go back and back to the woods unsatisfied, longing to express something that is there and not able to find it? This I know, I shall not find it until it comes out of my inner self.

In the years to come Emily would leave this landscape many more times, in search of her destiny in distant places across the world, until she finally reached the destination she had always sought, in the most unlikely of places—at home.

CHAPTER FOUR

A Student of Art

By the time she was eighteen, Emily knew she wanted to be an artist. She also knew that she had no real training or much exposure to art and artists. There were no museums or galleries in Victoria, and artists seldom visited. The few painters who had stopped in the city, the ones that Emily knew about, had given her a glimpse of a wider world. Just a glimpse, but enough for her to know there was more out there than she would find at home. She was not yet an artist, but she had desire, and desire is what counts.

She would have preferred to study in Europe—a couple of older acquaintances from her sketching group had already embarked for Paris and London—but in the family's eyes she was an unsophisticated girl without parental supervision, and Europe was a long way from the watchful gaze of her sisters. Emily was anxious not only to study art, but also to escape from the stifling, pious, strife-filled presence of her sisters, and especially from Edith, who was the authority in the house now.

Emily appealed to the family guardian. A decision was made that she would go to the art school in San Francisco. The Carrs had a long connection with the city. There were relatives and acquaintances in San Francisco with whom Emily could board, and who would keep an eye on her in what was considered to be something of a wicked place.

Even with an education, the options for a young woman in Emily's position were severely limited. Without the necessary schooling, she could not find employment in the usual occupations open to women—teaching, nursing, or secretarial work. But, with a course of study in art, she would at least be qualified to teach privately, if only to children or to other young ladies. This last fact might have prompted her guardian and her sisters to agree to the trip.

She arrived after a three-day voyage, a shy, inexperienced, naïve young woman, and before long settled down to a routine of study. Her drive, her dedication, and her capacity for hard work were soon evident. Like her desire, this dedication would never leave her.

In the classroom, she studied what every art student had always studied. Before brush could touch canvas, one first had to learn drawing. She was taught how to use a line and how to shade a mass. The models were still-life arrangements or plaster casts of the great sculptures from antiquity. As well, there were lessons in composition and perspective. Once a student had mastered the basics, she could progress to portraiture and drawing the figure. Emily's innate modesty, coupled with the rather puritanical attitude to the body that she had grown up with, made her avoid the classes on drawing and painting the nude or semi-nude model. She much preferred the outdoor landscape painting sessions, when the students left the city and set up their easels in a field or on a riverbank. Emily would find herself in classrooms many more times in the coming years, and always she would forsake them for study out of doors. Even in her first real art school, just a beginner, she was already a landscape painter at heart.

There were other young people in the classes, and Emily soon made friends. She joined a music club and took up the guitar. There were also a few lessons she learned outside the classroom that had nothing to do with art. She had been warned by Mrs. Piddington, who ran the residence where Emily lived, about opium dens in Chinatown, kidnappings, and white slavery. Once, with a friend, Emily wandered into a red-light district by accident and had the briefest of glimpses of the underside of San Francisco. Another friend seemed to lead a mysterious, sinful existence outside the classroom, and Emily was warned against associating with her. Some time after Emily returned to Victoria, she received news that this friend had died in compromising circumstances, possibly from the consequences of a mishandled abortion.

After she had been in San Francisco for a year, Emily's sisters arrived, and she went to live with them. Her brother, Dick, had left school in Ontario and was now in a sanatorium in Santa Barbara, ill with tuberculosis.

All the old tensions between Emily and Edith surfaced again. Emily was frustrated by the restrictions Edith imposed on her and realized how much she had enjoyed her independence. In 1893 an economic downturn hit the West Coast, and the combined expense of keeping Dick in the sanatorium and supporting Emily in San Francisco forced the family to call her back to Victoria.

Emily returned to Victoria not quite an artist, but no longer a student. There were practical lessons she had learned about techniques and methods during her studies, but she had also discovered that she could be independent, that she had talent, and that with hard work she might succeed in becoming an artist.

Once at home again, Emily did exactly what was expected of her: she set up a studio in the barn and advertised for pupils. Soon she had a barn full of children, and by all accounts she was a popular and successful teacher. Her playful side came out in the company of children and the classes were unconventional, especially since Emily always had a menagerie of small animals and birds in the barn. Nobody, especially her sisters, thought of her as a real artist. To them she was still little Milly. And if she thought of herself as an artist, she was one without a style or a subject. The works she made at this time were mostly in pencil and watercolour, in a realistic style that could best be described as conventional and picturesque.

During this period Emily made a visit to the Native village of Ucluelet, midway up the coast of Vancouver Island. The experience was a significant one, in ways that would affect her destiny, but this would become apparent only much later. In the meantime, Emily decided to become a student once again.

CHAPTER FIVE

A Canadian Abroad

In Victoria everyone who was anyone, or wanted to be someone, had either been born in England or had lived there, or traced their origins to Britain. England was where the news, fashions, ideas, culture, and sometimes even the food, originated. Important decisions were made there. It was the centre of the British Empire. In most people's minds, Canada was just a colony, and Victoria a very remote part of that colony. England was the homeland.

Emily had been chastised by her family for not being serious, for playing at art. She realized that she had learned a little in San Francisco, but not much. If an artist wanted a real education and a reputation, she had to go to London and be accredited, approved, and celebrated there first before she would be accepted at home.

Armed with recommendations and letters of introduction, Emily set off alone for London at age twenty-seven. She was eager, ambitious, and determined to succeed. As she had done in San Francisco, Emily stayed with relatives, family acquaintances, or in boarding houses for ladies. She enrolled at the Westminster School of Art, which had been recommended as first-rate but had declined both in reputation and quality of instruction by the time Emily arrived. A photograph of Emily from the time shows a mature-looking, sturdy young woman, conservatively dressed in a woolen cape, with a tam-o'-shanter perched on her luxuriant head of dark hair.

She hated London. As someone who had grown up surrounded by gardens and woods, and with the ocean just nearby, she found the city cramped and airless—not to mention dirty, crowded, noisy, and squalid. The studios at the school seemed to encapsulate everything that was disagreeable about the city. One of the few places she found relief was in Kew Gardens, not only because it was a place to escape the grimy confines of the city, but also because the gardens contained pine and cedar trees from British Columbia.

Instruction at the Westminster School was conservative and dull, a repetition of what Emily had studied in San Francisco, but this time she conquered her reservations about sketching from the nude model and enrolled in the life-drawing class. She visited the National Gallery and the British Museum, but the masterpieces she saw apparently made little impression on her. Her heart was still in the wilds of British Columbia. There were various other, more personal pressures upon Emily as well. News arrived that her brother, Dick, had died in California. Then a man she had established a friendship with in Victoria, and with whom she had maintained a correspondence, arrived in London and proposed marriage. Other suitors also offered her their hand. Even the doctor she had met on the ship from Canada courted her with a visit. But she declined them all. Lonely, out of place, oppressed by the city, she fell into a depression. Her health suffered and, finally, she became seriously ill.

Respite came when she quit both her classes and London, and left for the countryside. There she recovered her health and her spirits, even though she found the English countryside merely pretty and tame compared with the wild grandeur of British Columbia. In St. Ives, Cornwall, a coastal town popular with artists, she enrolled in outdoor painting classes. It was not to the picturesque fishing boats and beaches that she was drawn, however, but to the woods outside town. There, a sympathetic teacher encouraged her to look more deeply than she was accustomed to doing, and she at last began to learn something that she considered useful. Her teacher favoured the pastoral English landscape tradition, but showed her how to note the play of light and dark in the woods, to look for colour in the shadows, and to see not only the trees but the spaces between the trunks and foliage as well. These were lessons that Emily would long remember, and apply.

All was not work, however. There were trips around England, and she made many friends, often staying with them at their houses, once in a mansion in fashionable Belgravia.

Emily finally had to return to London. Once again she was lonely, feeling out of place and condescended to, both as a woman and as someone from the colonies. At the same time, her relatives were still pressuring her to marry and settle down. She had not made the breakthrough or achieved the success she had staked so much on. The city became unbearable. Emily suffered a complete physical and psychological collapse. Her sister Lizzie arrived and spent some time caring for her, but eventually a specialist was consulted. He diagnosed Emily's condition as a nervous breakdown.

She spent a year and a half recuperating at a sanatorium in the countryside. When Emily was finally well again, she packed her bags and departed for Canada. She had been five years in England, and was returning with neither reputation nor success to show for her efforts. Later in her life, when she came to write about this period in her autobiography, she would call it "A Pause." But at that moment, in her own eyes, and no doubt in the eyes of those who awaited her in Victoria, she was a failure.

CHAPTER SIX

Vancouver

Emily did not meet with the expected derision when she arrived home in Victoria. In fact, there was even a welcoming article on the front page of a local newspaper, lauding her return from studying under the "English Masters." Nevertheless, she was expected now to start a career and earn her own living.

Victoria was growing into a small city. Automobiles were appearing among the horse-drawn carriages. The Songhees reserve had been relocated away from the town to the Esquimault area. James Bay, where the Carr house was situated, had developed into a residential neighbourhood. The bridge across which her father had walked to his warehouse was replaced by a causeway when part of the bay was filled in. The Empress Hotel was being built in its place of dominance over the Inner Harbour.

For eight months in 1905, Emily put her talents to use drawing political cartoons for the Victoria publication *The Week*. Her humour, and her evident graphic skills, show that she could easily have pursued a career as an illustrator. But, determined as ever to follow her own path, she relocated to Vancouver, and once more set up as a teacher of art.

Her first job was at the Vancouver Studio Club, but she found the society ladies she was teaching to be mere hobbyists and amateurs, more interested in socializing than learning. The classes she held for children in her studio were much more satisfying. They were popular, too, and soon she had as many as seventy-five paying students. On the weekends Emily returned to the family home in Victoria, but now with an increasing reputation as a teacher, and her own income.

In Vancouver, Stanley Park occupies a peninsula that juts out from the western edge of the city, encompassing an area of some four hundred hectares. In Emily's day it was mostly an undeveloped wilderness of forest and beaches, with a few winding paths and tracks among the giant trees. It was there that Emily began to paint her first forest interiors.

The watercolour paintings she made in the park in 1909 and 1910 retain the naturalistic style she had learned in England. To the modern eye, they appear all drab browns and washed-out greens. The colour is descriptive rather than expressive, and the composition is uninspired. But there is something there, a spark and glimmer in the silence and the shadows, the genesis of what would one day flower.

During the summer of 1907, at the age of thirty-six, Emily took a cruise to Alaska with her sister Alice. In the town of Sitka and in a nearby Tlingit village, she saw for the first time the totem poles that would come to be her overriding subject. She had been to the Native settlement in Ucluelet twice already, but this was the first time she had seen anything like the carved poles and the painted house fronts. The watercolours she made on this trip, and subsequently on two more trips up the coast from Victoria, show flashes of unexpected colour and vitality, as if she had at last found a subject that she was inspired to paint.

In her autobiography, *Growing Pains,* she said of her exposure to the totem poles:

> Indian Art broadened my seeing, loosened the formal tightness I had learned in England's school. Its bigness and stark reality baffled my white man's understanding. I was as Canadian-born as the Indian, but behind me were Old World heredity and ancestry as well as Canadian environment.

It was during these trips that Emily began to formulate an ambitious project. Most people believed that totem poles would soon disappear as Native peoples adapted to the pressure to assimilate. The tradition of totem-carving seemed to be vanishing, and the remaining poles were either being abandoned to the elements or removed by collectors. Emily decided to make a visual record of the poles and carved figures in their original settings. The project did not come to fruition for some time, though. Just when she had found a subject for her painting, Emily, incredibly, decided to go back to being a student.

Perhaps she found her technique and abilities inadequate for representing the totem poles. No doubt she also had heard from artists with wider contacts in the world at large about a new kind of painting coming out of France—a new art that offered a new way of seeing. "I learned a lot from the Indians," she wrote later in her autobiography, "but who except Canada herself could help me comprehend her great woods and spaces? San Francisco had not, London had not. What about this New Art Paris talked of? It claimed bigger, broader seeing."

In the summer of 1910, accompanied by her sister Alice, Emily sailed for Paris.

CHAPTER SEVEN

In the French Style

When Emily Carr arrived in Paris, a revolution had taken place. Not in the streets, but in the studios of the artists.

Paris was the capital of the art world, and every ambitious painter set off to follow the same route to success. The path to accomplishment had been laid out for a long time: first study at the École Nationale Supérieure des Beaux-Arts, then exhibit at the Salon (the annual exhibition organized by the Académie des Beaux-Arts), receive prestigious commissions from the state or the Church, and finally, become a member of the academy and enjoy the fruits of success.

The kinds of subject matter suitable for painting had also been codified and followed a strict hierarchy: religious, historical, or classical subjects first; then portraiture and figure paintings; lastly, genres such as still life or domestic interiors. Paintings were expected to be as realistic as possible and done with a flawless finish. Landscape as a subject in itself was considered inconsequential, unless it included a significant monument or referred to the above-mentioned subjects.

Artists had always made outdoor sketches, but these were considered mere practice or studies, not finished paintings. The revolution in painting took place when artists rejected the authority of both the Salon and the Academy, as well as the hierarchy of subjects. In the early and mid-nineteenth century, painters increasingly began to turn away from the accepted subjects and to paint the world around them, including the countryside outside Paris. Two factors, among many others, contributed to this change: the newly developed railways that made travel to the outlying regions easily possible, and a change in the technology of artists' materials.

A painter usually had to mix dry pigment with oil to obtain a workable paint. The process could be undertaken properly only in the studio and was messy and time-consuming. When ready-to-use paints in portable tubes were introduced, all a painter had to do was pack them into a paintbox, take along a foldable easel and lunch, and he could spend a day painting in the countryside and still catch a train home in time for dinner.

Using the new ready-mixed colours, painters worked rapidly out of doors. Instead of the smooth, blended surface that viewers were accustomed to seeing, painters began to use short brush strokes of pure colour placed next to each other, based on an optical theory that suggested the eye would do the mixing. So, for instance, an impression of green could be achieved by laying dabs and strokes of yellow and blue together. The same green could be obtained by actually mixing the two pigments into each other on the palette, but the new method gave new vibrancy and brightness to the painting.

For artists, painting out of doors, creating a subjective impression of what they saw instead of a realistic copy of a scene, and considering these paintings not as sketches but as completed works of art, became valid and accepted practice.

The artists who worked in this style were called the Impressionists, and today they are household names. The style eventually spread across Europe and to North America. Various stylistic developments took place, as Monet and Renoir were followed by Gauguin and Van Gogh, and then Matisse, Picasso, and others. Each new style built on the previous ones: Expressionism, Fauvism, Symbolism, and Cubism, eventually leading to the abstractions of modernism. This new way of seeing and painting can, for convenience, be called Post-Impressionism, and that was what Emily Carr had come to learn when she arrived in Paris in 1910.

Emily had already glimpsed the new styles in the work that her friend, Theresa Wylde, had brought back from France. And in the painted totem poles of the Native peoples she had seen a use of colour and line that was radically different from what she had learned so far. There were other artists in Canada working in the Impressionist vein. In Ontario, young painters like Tom Thomson, Lawren Harris, and A.Y. Jackson would eventually think about how to apply this new style to Canadian subject matter.

When Emily enrolled in one of the private Parisian academies, it seemed like a step backward, a return to the usual drawing from the model, studying composition and perspective, copying plaster casts. She had done all this already in San Francisco and London. At the age of forty, she no longer had time to repeat a basic art education. For a period, it seemed as if France would be a failure, just as London had been. The city oppressed her. She was dissatisfied with the instruction at the academy. She felt isolated and lonely. Illness, both emotional and physical, threatened to curtail her efforts.

Relief came when she followed one of her teachers to study out of doors on the coast of Brittany. Emily's work blossomed. The colours brightened; details were suppressed in favour of the overall effect; a freedom and confidence was evident in the way she used her brush. Gone were the muted landscapes of the English style. When Emily showed her teacher some of her sketches of Native subjects, they were praised, and she even repainted one or two of the sketches in the new style.

A word or two should be said about how a single woman in Emily's circumstances travelled and lived in the year 1911. She was not alone, but journeyed to Paris with her sister Alice, who had learned some French. While not rich, the sisters had ample funds for a comfortable journey, and were prepared with letters of introduction and a list of acquaintances and friends or relatives to call on.

The rail trip across Canada from Vancouver took a leisurely three weeks, with visits to Banff and Calgary, a stay of a week in Edmonton, and twelve days in Quebec City. The sisters left from there on an eight-day sea voyage and disembarked in Liverpool. A short stay in London ensued before they crossed the English Channel to Le Havre and took the train to Paris.

They rented an apartment on Boulevard Raspail in the Montparnasse neighbourhood. Nearby were the cafés where the young artists like Picasso and Modigliani were debating the latest theories about art. Gertrude Stein's weekly salons, where the avant-garde of the literary and artistic worlds met, were a regular event not too far away.

Emily, however, lived in a completely different milieu. Despite her ambitions as an artist, she was still a conventional middle-class lady from Victoria. Her teachers and the artists she visited were British. Her social life took place entirely within an English-speaking expatriate group. The only café she frequented was the tea room in the American Student Hostel Club on the Boulevard Saint-Michel. The club offered visits to museums and galleries, and no doubt Emily saw the sights on group tours, but whether or not she saw any of the avant-garde art being produced in the neighbourhood is impossible to know.

She worked hard, enrolled in both day and night classes. The pressure took its toll. She began to suffer crippling headaches, as she had done before in London. The old family strife erupted between her and Alice. The city was noisy, cramped, and dirty. After three months Emily fell ill, and in what seems like a repetition of her London experience, spent six weeks at the American Student Hostel infirmary. After a brief period of convalescence in the apartment she had a relapse, and returned for another stay in the infirmary. When she recovered sufficiently the two sisters travelled to Gothenburg, Sweden, where Emily had a friend and where Alice, the teacher, could study the Swedish school system. Emily slowly regained her strength at a seaside spa.

On their return to Paris, instead of resuming studio classes, Emily followed one of her teachers, William Phelan "Harry" Gibb, to a village two hours by rail from Paris, where he was giving outdoor classes in landscape painting. She took a room in the house of Gibb and his wife Bridget, while Alice remained at the apartment in Paris. When the Gibbs moved in the summer to Brittany, Emily did too, taking lodgings in a hotel nearby.

Alice returned to Canada. Yet Emily was not lonely. She was happy in the little villages where she found that the peasants, and their quiet, dignified way of life, reminded her of the Natives she had met in Canada. Gibb taught her a great deal in the daily lessons that took place in the fields and hills. And he praised her work, going so far as to tell her that she would become one of the great painters of her time—*women* painters, he added.

We should not imagine that Emily was isolated during her studies in Brittany. Ever since Gauguin and Van Gogh had made the area popular, artists' colonies had become a fixture up and down the coast. Many of the artists gave classes, and the hotels were full of international visitors. Emily's landscape paintings from this period, like *Trees in France* (1911), show not only how fluent she had become in the colourful new style—trees outlined in red, shadows of violet and blue, grass of pure orange—but also that even then her best work was being done when she used the woods as her subject matter.

When the Gibbs returned to Paris Emily stayed on, moving along the coast to the town of Concarneau, where she studied for six weeks with Frances Hodgkins, a New Zealand artist. Hodgkins was the only woman Emily ever had as a teacher. Her significant teachers and mentors would always be men.

The meeting between the two women provides an interesting footnote in the life of Emily Carr. Hodgkins and Emily were of a similar age, both single women who had refused proposals of marriage, both transplanted from the outer reaches of the British Empire. Frances had supported herself in New Zealand through teaching and illustration, and had a local reputation based on her paintings of the Maori natives. She was an independent woman and ambitious to develop as a painter. Finding life in her town of Dunedin too confining, she had come to Europe, and like Emily, had been in London and Cornwall to study. Finding New Zealand still unsatisfactory when she returned, Hodgkins had come to France in 1906 to learn with the moderns. Also, like Emily, she found cities stifling and had settled in Brittany. In France, both women found that although they were considered foreigners, they were not looked down upon as colonials. Unlike Emily, who always felt that she belonged only in Victoria, Frances would remain in Europe, and later achieved a reputation in England.

The culmination of Emily's sojourn in France came on the day in 1911 when she walked down the Champs-Élysées to the annual Salon d'Automne at the Grand Palais. There, two of her works, which had been submitted by Harry Gibb, were accepted to hang among the most daring and innovative artists of her time.

When she departed for Canada, it was not only as an accomplished painter, but also as a modern artist.

CHAPTER EIGHT

The Wild Beast

The style of painting that Emily had learned in France is generally called Post-Impressionism, but it would be more accurate to label it Fauve. In French, the word means literally "wild beast," and was the derogatory term used by an unsympathetic critic to characterize the artists whose use of pure, bright colour struck him as savage and crude.

As soon as she re-established herself in a Vancouver studio in 1912, Emily held an exhibition of the works she had painted in France. The newspaper reviews were polite but befuddled. Except for a few artist friends, the reaction of those who came to see the new works ranged from confusion to hostility. The paintings were derided as uncouth and primitive, and some of her supporters urged her to return to a style that people could more easily understand. Sales were practically nonexistent and Emily found it difficult to resume teaching. She was an avant-garde painter now, but she was alone, one of the few modernist painters in the entire country. Not even the Group of Seven would make such daring use of colour and form until almost a decade later.

Undeterred, Emily turned to the grand project she had postponed when she left for France: she set out to make a record for posterity of the totem poles of the West Coast. She undertook an ambitious, six-week-long journey north and east to the interior of British Columbia, painting everywhere she stopped. Now she had the understanding and the technique to paint, not as a camera would record, but as an artist would see. The word "Indian" began to be associated with her name, as Native motifs were now the exclusive subject of her paintings. A certain notoriety began to attach itself to her reputation.

In 1912 Emily approached the provincial government with the suggestion that they purchase the collection as a historical record, and help fund her future trips, for the project was by no means completed. An expert was sent to look at the work and make an assessment. While he was sympathetic, his report indicated that her paintings were not suitable as an ethnographic record. Her colours were too vivid, and her style too expressive, for the works to accurately reflect the true nature of the poles and sites. The government turned down Emily's offer. It was a short-sighted decision. Even if the pictures don't conform to strict anthropological criteria, they would indeed have been a significant collection for posterity. Other than her paintings and some historical photographs, there is no documentation of the places she visited. And, just as she anticipated, many of the poles have weathered and disintegrated or been removed to other places.

Surprisingly, Emily became friends with the expert sent to evaluate the paintings, C.F. Newcombe, a physician and anthropologist, who seems to have sympathized with and encouraged her interests. In 1913 Emily rented a hall in Vancouver and presented an exhibition of the paintings, almost two hundred of them. She even gave a public lecture in an attempt to explain her project.

The response to the exhibition was similar to that which greeted her French pictures. Again she met with ridicule, ignorance, and hostility that, because of the subject matter, was sometimes thinly disguised racism. Certainly, a painting like *The Welcome Man* (1913) would have disconcerted an audience. The sky and sea are lemon yellow, the distant mountains are purple, and the dark silhouette of a carved figure in the foreground looms over the viewer. The picture has the same power as the Norwegian Expressionist Edvard Munch's brooding Nordic landscapes. No doubt it would have disturbed and terrified visitors looking for some nice views of the picturesque coast. What they got instead was the raw, emotive power of art.

The tremendous change in Emily's style is apparent in a comparison of two paintings of the same scene, one done in 1908 and the other in 1912. The earlier work, showing two war canoes on the shore of Alert Bay, is mostly painted in washed-out browns. The only bit of colour is on the hulls of the canoes. The later picture, a double-sized version of the same scene, has emerald streaks in the hills and the water; a flash of bright red shows in a tree trunk next to deep violet; the sky vibrates with yellow and light turquoise brush strokes. Viewers of her new paintings might not have liked them, but there was no denying their originality and power.

But mostly there was silence. All artists at some point ask themselves what use their work is to the world. If Emily thought she had found a use for herself and her talent, she was disappointed. An artist can fight against resistance; some even thrive on it. But to be ignored is the worst response of all.

This time Emily bowed her head in defeat. She gave up her Vancouver studio, returned to Victoria, ceased her sketching trips up the coast, and abandoned her grand project. In *Growing Pains,* she titled the chapter detailing this period with one word: "Rejected."

During the next decade she would make very few paintings, and those she did create are notable for the complete absence of Native motifs.

CHAPTER NINE

How to Be a Woman

Emily Carr was once offered a job. The job description was straightforward and unambiguous.

She was required to do the grocery shopping; to prepare, cook, and serve the food; and then to wash the dishes after meals. She would also have to host occasional dinner parties. She would do the sweeping, scrubbing, and polishing to keep up the house. Laundry would have to be washed, dried, ironed, and folded. She would also be responsible for the household accounts and would have to balance the books. In the garden, she would see to the flowers and grow vegetables. In addition, she would have to bear, raise, feed, and care for children. At all times she would be required to be kind, capable, amusing, loving, and attractive.

The job offer came in the form of a marriage proposal when she was twenty-eight. Emily declined the offer, and all others. By choosing art over marriage, she made a momentous decision. In her journals she said of the man who had proposed: "He demanded more than I could have given him. He demanded worship. He thought I made a great mistake in not marrying him. He ought to be glad I did not: he'd have found me a bitter mouthful and very indigestible, and he would have bored me till my spirit died."

In one of those terrible ironies that fate sometimes deals, Emily later had to undertake many of those same household tasks when she ran a boarding house and served as housekeeper and mother to a disparate and changing group of tenants.

Because she was a woman, and an unconventional one, Emily always struggled against the expectations and prejudice of men, as well as other women, both as an artist and an individual. More than anything, she wanted to be an artist. There shouldn't have been anything wrong with that ambition. Artistic flair was considered an asset in a woman. The ability to sketch, along with some musical ability, and perhaps an aptitude to write light verse, added to a woman's attractiveness. And if a woman did persist in painting, the subjects thought suitable for her talents were flowers, children, small animals, and delicate landscapes in watercolour.

The language used to describe women was also applied to their art: delicate, graceful, charming, modest, sensitive—a language of passivity.

A career as a professional artist just was not considered suitable for a lady. Men could marry and remain artists. Women were expected to be wives and mothers, and little else. A man could be an artist and remain a bachelor, but an unmarried woman was pitied as a spinster. Even in Paris and London, where artistic milieus existed that were opening to women, an artist's prospects were still determined, in part, by gender.

Many young women did go to art school. In fact, they tended to dominate in numbers, but as students only, very seldom as teachers. Most never came near to being artists. The only outlet they could find for their talents was as teachers in the regular school system. And if they did form clubs and arts organizations, the names were always prefixed by the words "Ladies" or "Women's." Men gave their clubs and organizations more important titles, like Academy, Salon, or Royal Society. And if women were given the opportunity to study in these academies and societies, it often was in segregated classes. The histories of art written at the time made absolutely no mention of a single woman artist.

When women's art was reviewed in the newspapers, as Emily's was, the articles generally appeared in the women's section. When Emily held an exhibition of her work from France, the paintings were discussed in the Vancouver

Province on the page for "Casual Comment on Women's Activities and Interests," alongside articles on fashion and social gossip. Men's art was never relegated to a page otherwise devoted to carpentry and fishing.

Higher education was effectively closed to women. They were not accepted into most faculties at most universities. Women lawyers, judges, physicians, or engineers simply did not exist. Other than taking menial jobs, they could be typists, secretaries, or clerks. Women did not live alone or travel without a chaperone, and to be unmarried past a certain age carried a social stigma that veered between pity and condemnation. In Canada, women were barred from voting both provincially and federally until 1917–18.

When the Group of Seven painters began to achieve some positive notice after 1920, they were often portrayed in heroic terms as brave Canadian artists. But when a handful of serious and talented women—contemporaries of Emily's, if only in age—formed the Beaver Hall Group in Montreal at around the same time, they received nothing like the attention devoted to the Group of Seven, even though they were accomplished painters working in the progressive styles. It is worth noting that of the ten women in the Beaver Hall group, only one married, and only briefly.

The artistic climate in Victoria, what little there was of it, remained conservative throughout Emily's lifetime. Art was more often than not displayed at annual fairs along with handicrafts, agricultural products, and horticultural exhibits. The society in which Emily lived viewed art, especially the modern variety, with suspicion, and saw its practitioners as social outsiders, unless they had been lauded already in the dominant European institutions. A modern artist who made no sales and received no commissions was beyond the pale. Because women's roles were so circumscribed and the expectations of how they should act were so defined, a woman like Emily, who flouted conventional expectations and persisted in working as an artist in the modern vein, was bound to be viewed as an oddity.

She had certain other "bad" characteristics. She smoked cigarettes. She used strong language. She played cards. She rode a horse astride, like a man, instead of sidesaddle, like a polite young woman. She had a monkey as a pet. Then there were her friends. She championed a Chinese artist who had been rejected by a local art society because of his race. She often visited a man confined to a lunatic asylum. She took a mentally handicapped boy along on a few of her local sketching excursions. She formed a friendship with a Native woman who was considered an alcoholic prostitute.

And then there were the Indians. It was bad enough that she painted images of what was considered a savage and primitive art form. But Emily went further than that; she actually went to live among the Native people on her trips and slept in their houses. Conventional observers saw this behaviour as a betrayal of all the civilizing virtues for which their society stood.

Emily was independent, forthright in her views, and had a healthy disrespect for the established order. Some of her contemporaries considered her selfish, egotistical, and irritable, qualities accepted in a man but deemed unfeminine in a woman. We could also say that she was ambitious, dedicated, hardworking, and didn't suffer fools gladly, but local society had already filed her away in the category of outsider and eccentric.

Male artists were allowed to be eccentric, bad-tempered, or sexually profligate. Such traits were often attributed to their creative temperament, and might even be seen as a sign of genius. A woman who exhibited the same traits was considered mentally unbalanced.

It is tempting, in retrospect, to see Emily Carr as an early feminist. She wasn't—at least in the political sense of the term. Although the movement for equal rights for women was well underway in Canada by the 1920s, her diaries make barely a reference to any political events of the day. In 1917 a suffragette demonstration in Victoria was disrupted by police, but the event seems to have made no impression on Emily. Margaret Clay, a politically active friend and supporter, visited Emily frequently in the 1920s and 1930s, but Emily never participated in Margaret's activities. Emily was opinionated, but she was always aware of her lack of formal education, and tended to be reticent when conversation took an intellectual turn. She was a feminist in the personal sphere only: she was always determined to make her own choices without having to defer to the opinions of others.

Neither was Carr anti-male. She had a number of significant platonic friendships with men. She preferred the company of women, but in her professional life she responded to the advice of men. This comes as no surprise, considering the authority men wielded both in society and the arts, but we must remember also that she had grown up in a household of women whose wills were ultimately subordinate to that of Richard Carr.

To see Carr as an entirely rejected and isolated woman is inaccurate. Her artistic contacts with the mainstream in Canada and elsewhere were sporadic, but she did have the company of other artists in Victoria and Vancouver, and had her supporters among them. She exhibited frequently, albeit in minor venues or in her own studios. She had a great many friends and relatives, as well as the constant company of her sisters, and in most respects lived a fully integrated social life. The fact that she was an unconventional and independent artist, frustrated in her ambitions and development, often led Emily to portray herself as lonely and isolated. There is truth in that self-characterization, but only to a degree.

CHAPTER TEN

Female Hysteria

Emily was not physically weak. She undertook arduous sketching trips and engaged in strenuous physical labour during her years as a landlady. Nevertheless, she suffered from a variety of ailments over the course of her life, one severe enough to confine her to a sanatorium for fifteen months.

In 1900, shortly after she arrived in London, one of her big toes was amputated when it did not heal properly after a carriage accident in Canada. Just before her scheduled departure for Paris in 1910, she contracted diphtheria and was confined to bed for weeks. In Paris she became ill with what she described as either bronchitis or jaundice. Twice she spent periods of about six weeks in the American Student Hostel infirmary, and eventually she travelled with her sister Alice to a spa in Sweden, where she recovered. In her forties she had a gall bladder operation that was apparently unsuccessful. Finally, in her later years, she was felled by two heart attacks and two strokes, the combination of which caused her death.

Throughout her life she suffered from periods of depression, and her journals frequently refer to the black moods that sent her to bed in despair. But it was during her stay in England that a combination of physical and psychological disorders resulted in a complete breakdown. Her toe took a long time to heal and must certainly have been painful. She received news of the death from tuberculosis of her brother, Dick, in California. At the same time, a suitor, Mayo Paddon, was visiting and importuning her to marry him. She began to suffer debilitating headaches and nausea. Emily actually collapsed when she and Alice were among the crowd watching the funeral procession for Queen Victoria, the first sign that her health was in a precarious state. She found London oppressive and confining, but a summer in the country brought no respite from the headaches. In Cornwall, where she went to attend sketching classes, the glaring light on the beach made her flee into the shade of the woods, angering her teacher.

Before returning to London she spent a period in a nursing home trying to regain her energy, but when she did go back to the city she again suffered fainting spells, accompanied by numbness in her right arm and leg. A friend in the country took her in for just over a month. No record of a diagnosis exists, but it was likely that the strenuous effort she made at her work, knowing how much rode on her success, coupled with the effects of the surgery on her foot, contributed to her constant bouts of illness. The headaches and nausea probably had a physical cause, migraine perhaps, but the only advice she received was to rest.

In July 1902, Emily's sister Lizzie arrived in England. Unable to bear a return to the city, which she saw as a prison, Emily moved to a succession of lodgings outside London. She would recover, and then a relapse would come. Her symptoms included fits of stuttering, heart palpitations, and numbness on one side. A specialist was consulted. He concluded that she was suffering from a nervous breakdown.

Eventually, in January 1903, Emily was admitted to a sanatorium in Suffolk. She would remain there until March of the following year.

Women's health problems tended to be under-diagnosed and were often dismissed as psychosomatic under the general heading of "female hysteria." (Male hysteria, which usually manifests itself in wars and sports, has of course never been considered a psychosis.) The origin of the illness was often attributed to sexual repression and familial conflicts, which were converted into physical symptoms. The growing popularity of Sigmund Freud's pseudo-scientific speculations encouraged the view that women were sexually repressed. This repression was attributed neither to male domination nor societal strictures, but instead to supposedly unconscious fantasies. Among the alleged fantasies were feelings of sexual attraction to the father, resulting in such severe anxiety that impairment of speech and limb might result.

A number of later writers have applied these imaginative speculations to Emily Carr's breakdown, equating her refusal to marry with sexual frigidity or unacknowledged homosexuality, or even to an actual sexual encounter with her own father. Such judgments are perhaps too easy to make upon a woman who consciously violated conventional rules of behaviour.

What is more likely is that Emily was suffering from specific physical ailments that were left unattended. Her psychological breakdown could just as easily have been a result of the enormous pressure she put on herself. She was thirty-three in 1904, older than most other students in the classes she attended. She knew that her family and her acquaintances in Victoria expected her to succeed, perhaps as her old friend Sophie Pemberton had done—with success at the Royal Academy and further triumph in Paris. Pemberton was a talented painter in the Beaux-Arts tradition, but the kind of art Emily wanted to make had no tradition. As well, the Carr sisters had allocated family funds to Emily's continuing education and she did not want to disappoint them.

Emily felt alone and out of place in England. She was slighted as a "colonial," and she longed for the landscape of home. Yet she had to stay. To leave would be to admit failure. Finally, she was still considered eligible for marriage, and relatives in England constantly tried to pair her off with suitable men. The combination of all these factors, along with exhaustion and ill health, broke her down.

The treatment for the breakdown was dubious, to say the least. The medical establishment was as ignorant as Emily herself as to what ailed her. She was kept on a strict diet, then was switched to a different one that made her gain weight. There were experimental electric massages and enforced bed rest. Stimulation of any kind was discouraged, and she was forbidden to paint or even to think about it. In her memoir Emily wrote that she felt like a vegetable at this time, living in an uneventful forever and forever. What kept her sane were the satirical sketches and verses she made up, and the little birds she raised in her room.

That Emily did not succumb, either to the diagnosis or the treatment, but returned to her grand ambition, is a testament not so much to her physical strength as to the deep resources of inner courage she possessed.

CHAPTER ELEVEN

The Edge of Nowhere

Emily once referred to herself as a little old lady on the edge of nowhere. But she was a great traveller. She saw more of Canada and parts of Europe than the majority of people of her time and class, and more than many of us have done, even today.

Although Victoria was always her home, and she never lived more than a few blocks from where she had been born, throughout her life she regularly packed her bags and set off for distant locations. She took her first journey when she was twenty-two, and didn't unpack for the final time until she was in her sixties.

Here is a partial list of the places she visited: San Francisco, New York, Chicago, London, Cornwall, Paris, Brittany, Sweden, Toronto, Ottawa, Montreal, Quebec City, Edmonton, the Cariboo, Alaska, Seattle, various places in the British Columbia interior, the Queen Charlotte Islands, and then the many trips she made to Native villages and towns up and down the coast.

If all her sketching trips in British Columbia were compounded into one imaginary journey, it would go something like this: she begins her journey on a steamer from Victoria to Prince Rupert, a distance of five hundred kilometres. From Prince Rupert she heads inland, perhaps to Hazleton, another three hundred kilometres. First she travels by rail, and then by paddle steamer up the river for some distance. She then transfers to a smaller boat which takes her to a town. There she boards a horse-drawn cart, and sits among the lumber and sacks of oats for another journey of some hours. Once she reaches the village that is her destination, she hires a horse and rides farther inland until she reaches a smaller settlement. Here, where there are no more roads and tracks, she will have to progress onward by foot. She has brought with her a small folding stool, a bedroll, some canned provisions, and a canvas sheet that functions as a kind of tent when it rains. She also carries her paintbox containing small canvas panels and her brushes and paints.

This journey is not accomplished all in one continuous sequence. Emily breaks up the trip with stopovers, during which she stays with relatives, friends, missionaries, and Indian agents. The accommodation varies. Sometimes it's a small hotel, a borrowed cottage, a lighthouse, an abandoned school, or a Native longhouse. It all depends on who her host of the moment is. She sketches the people and the landscapes she visits, producing some of her most interesting work, from a historical perspective.

She travels alone, but she is not alone. Always she has her little dog for company, and there are guides along the way, sometimes a fisherman, or a Native couple she hires to transport her in their boat, or a young Native girl who is sent to show her a path into the forest.

Sometimes she is frightened. On one occasion, she imagines that she has been abandoned on a beach where a fisherman has left her. He promised to return in a few hours, but then a storm blows up, and she must huddle in her tent waiting to be rescued. Often, when she is alone in the forest, she imagines a wild animal seizing her from behind. Sometimes it is just the eerie silence that gives her what she calls the "creeps," so far from human voices, a thousand kilometres from home. But she perseveres.

The mist blows in from the unseen ocean, moss droops from the trees, a brooding silence fills the spaces. She goes deeper into the forest, into the dense dark green of the shadows, where the only illumination is from the narrow shafts of sunlight that pierce the canopy high above her head.

She arrives at the totem poles that she has come to find. They are solemn and tall as the cedars from which they were carved, weathered by time, half obscured at the base by thick nettles. A peculiar feeling comes over her, a mixture of awe and fear at their strangeness. In her words, "The ferocious, strangled lonesomeness of that place . . . full of unseen things and great silence." Those carved and painted figures, are they human, are they animal, or something else altogether? She sees herself in the totem poles' faces, and she sees herself in the dark primeval forest, and for a moment she is terrified.

She unfolds her stool and sets up her paints, then she lights a cigarette to keep away the insects that have started to hover around her head. A kind of desolation hangs over the place, but also a beauty that she has found nowhere else, either in the docile English countryside or in the rocky coastal villages of Brittany. She has glimpsed the grandeur of Canadian landscapes in some paintings by Lawren Harris and his fellow artists in Toronto, but here in the West, no artist has painted this forest. That is why she has come to this place, to paint this terrible beauty.

A painting from 1931, *Strangled by Growth,* shows a carved face peering out of a swirling mass of greenery that is half garment and half light waves that have somehow become solid. The painting is very still and yet at the same time bursting with life.

All of these elements—the tree when it was growing, the carver who cut into the wood, the history and the myths and the people who once lived here—are in the painting. All of them and more: the slow invisible growth, the particles of dust, and the insects drifting in the shafts of sunlight, all are alive in some big way that she senses but cannot put into words. There is a force that pulses through everything. She feels it in her veins, in the beating of her heart, in the slow turning of the earth, and in the invisible stars in the sky. Not even the word "god" is big enough to encompass what she feels.

How to tell it? How to say it? How to touch it and show it? Emily speaks in the only way she can, with her brush. She dips it into the dabs of paint on her palette and makes a mark on the canvas—a gentle, rhythmic curve of green, a shape and a form and a feeling. There it is. And now, here in the great stillness on the edge of nowhere, she makes something for eternity.

CHAPTER TWELVE

The Great Stillness

I have on the desk in front of me a small sculpture, about twenty-five centimetres high, made of argillite, a black stone found in Haida Gwaii. The sculpture is a miniature totem pole, purchased for a few dollars in a tourist shop many years ago, as a souvenir of a visit to Vancouver's Stanley Park. The sculpture represents, as far as I can tell, an eagle, a frog, a bear, and at the very top, a small human face topped by a conical hat. The notice on the back explains: "Totem poles are visual representations of legends past. Each crest interwoven with one another symbolizes stories of mysticism, nature and man." Even though it is a mass-produced object for the tourist trade, and I am ignorant of the meanings of the creatures, it has a very powerful and distinctive presence.

The sculpture, which is similar to a model that Emily owned, reminds me a bit of Emily's paintings, particularly one called, simply, *Totem and Forest* (1931), where the totem with its compacted and dense representations of life rises, iconic and glowing, against the dense mass of the dark forest.

In 1907, after her years of art classes in England, Emily and Alice took a cruise up the coast to Alaska. On a stop of a few hours in the Kwakiutl village of Alert Bay, Emily saw totem poles for the first time. The sisters' destination was the town of Sitka, already something of a tourist spot, and there, in a wooded area known as Totem Walk, where totem poles of the Haida and Tlingit people had been re-erected for the tourists, Emily had a chance to make her first painting of totem poles in the forest.

The painting is a muted watercolour of a tree-lined path, mostly in browns and greens, and yet to one side is a brilliant splash of colour, red and blue and white with black lines—a totem pole, bright as a beacon in the shadows. She will come back to this motif again and again. In this small watercolour is the beginning of the great artist she will become.

At about this time, Emily also met an American artist, T.E. Richardson, who had spent numerous summers travelling to Native villages in Alaska to paint, and then selling the pictures in New York for handsome prices.

Anyone who has seen a totem pole, either in a museum or in a natural environment, can attest to its tremendous effect and presence. When Emily Carr saw them for the first time, their colours and shapes so vivid against the backdrop of the forest, she must have found them stunning. She had visited the Louvre in Paris and the British Museum in London, but had never encountered anything quite like this. She saw it as art, yes, but also as an expression of the place and the people who were of that place. What she saw was art with a purpose and an art of great originality. The common misperception among most non-Native people at this time was that the Aboriginal culture of the West Coast was declining, and that the totem poles were already disappearing. Emily probably had some inkling of the enormous transformations Native culture was being subjected to by white society, and this may have been why she undertook what she saw as a socially useful project: to make a visual record of the poles. Whatever her intention as a sort of amateur anthropologist, it was as an artist that she approached the project.

Emily embarked on her mission in the summer of 1908. In the years that followed she would return again and again to the forest, each time finding new subjects, new places, new techniques. When she came back from France, with a new, colourful palette and a different way of applying the paint, she would paint the poles and houses. Later, after her success at the National Gallery in 1927 and inspired by Lawren Harris and the Group of Seven, she would throw herself back into her sketching trips with a renewed passion, producing some of her finest paintings.

When her work entered a new stage, she abandoned Native motifs for a time and turned to pure landscape painting, but even then, at the very end of her career, she occasionally picked up one of her early sketches and worked it up into a finished painting. The chronology of her painting trips is the chronology of a journey, not only physical but also artistic, and it is the trajectory of a quest both to find and make meaning from what she found in the primeval forest.

But what are these totem poles, these carved and decorated tree trunks that became so important to her? What was their function? Who made them? What do they represent?

The totem poles of the West Coast Native peoples are unique. The geographical area where they are created is limited to the coastland from southern Alaska down to mid-British Columbia and does not extend much inland. As generally used in Native culture, a totem is an object or animal that is adopted as the emblem of an individual, family, or larger social group. It serves as an identifier and as a symbol of unity within the clan.

The European equivalent might be a heraldic crest or flag. Some scholars say that the term "crest poles" is more accurate. The crests belong to specific individuals and groups, and in that sense they are owned only by them. They are not works of art in the Western meaning of the term, although there is a creative and aesthetic aspect to their design. The images on the poles are drawn from the environment in which they are created and most often consist of animal motifs—raven, bear, salmon, eagle, frog—as well as human faces and mythological creatures.

Totem poles can be part of a ceremony. They can illustrate stories or personify elements in the mythology of the group. They can also mark territory or a burial place. Because the coastal peoples did not use a written language or make pictures, the poles are carriers of meaning and history.

Europeans began to collect and remove the totem poles and carved masks almost as soon as they encountered them. They took them as exotic curios, as souvenirs, as oddities, as objects for museums, and as items that could be sold. The Christian missionaries, who brought their own iconography in the symbol of the crucifix and in the tales collected in the Bible, saw the Native poles as a competing system of "heathen" beliefs. They made a concerted effort to shame the Natives into seeing their masks and totems as uncivilized and primitive. Totem poles were destroyed, abandoned, removed, and the art of carving was actively discouraged.

In 1894, under the Indian Act, the potlatch ceremony, in which masks and poles played a part, was banned by the government. The potlatch was a gathering of Native peoples that served many social purposes and functions. Economic and governance matters might be dealt with. Rites of passage, such as births and weddings, might be celebrated. Historical and spiritual rituals would be enacted. It was also an occasion of feasting and celebration. The potlatch strengthened relations between different tribes and confirmed Native identity as separate from that of the Europeans. Suppression of the potlatch also had the effect of making totem poles irrelevant to the lives of the Native peoples.

Because they are carved from trees, totem poles naturally decay and must be replaced by fresh ones. But the poles were losing their original function, and were reduced, through European intervention, to the archeological remnants of a dying culture. Many of the villages that Emily Carr visited had been abandoned for other reasons: either the inhabitants had been relocated under pressure to assimilate, or their traditional hunting and fishing practices had been disrupted, or the populations had died from the newly introduced diseases like smallpox and measles. The irony that some of the newcomers were trying to preserve the poles while others worked actively to destroy the culture that created them was lost on many people.

Emily might not have been aware of the political and cultural complexity of the situation, but she did see the changes taking place. As an artist, she was deeply affected by the power of the poles, and if only for that reason she felt compelled to make others aware of them, too. It was also through the totem poles that Emily found her identity as an artist, and through them she would find purpose and meaning in her life.

The argillite sculpture I have on my desk, although removed from its true meaning and context, still resonates not only with personal memories but also with deeper meanings that stretch back through time and connect me to Emily Carr, and then further back to the First Peoples who created the original totem poles, and through them even further into the great mystery that is life.

CHAPTER THIRTEEN

In the Wilderness

There are fallow periods in every creative person's life, when they lose faith in their endeavours and it seems as if all their efforts have come to nothing. The composer Richard Wagner went into exile for years and then emerged with the stunning Ring Cycle operas. After a lost election Winston Churchill retreated into political silence, a period he called "the wilderness years," before coming back to lead his country through the Second World War. Even the tremendously prolific Picasso was inactive for a couple of years, turning away from painting to take up poetry and playwriting instead. Adversity can silence the creative impulse, but the flame is never extinguished.

After 1913, Emily's grand project to record the Native totem poles for posterity had been abandoned. The exhibition of her French works had met with indifference and hostility and she was unable to resume her teaching positions in Vancouver. She retreated to Victoria, discouraged and depressed.

Meanwhile, there was a growing threat of war in Europe while, at home, an economic depression resulted in higher property taxes, unemployment, and inflation. The Carr family funds had shrunk over the years and the sisters were forced to sell off some of their land. The family home was rented out and the sisters built other accommodation for themselves. Emily had a house constructed next to Beacon Hill Park, with the idea of renting out part of it while setting aside a studio and apartment for herself. But long-term tenants were hard to come by in those unsettled years, so she took in boarders instead. The studio became a sitting-dining room for tenants and Emily made do with rooms in the attic for herself.

Two myths have arisen about this period in Emily's life: first, that she lived in dire poverty, and second, that she gave up painting entirely. Both are only partly true.

Although Emily owned land and the house, she had no regular income other than the rent she collected. Consequently, she took on the management of the boarding house herself. She did the repairs and maintenance, the finances, the cooking, and the washing. She even stoked the furnace with coal and shovelled snow in winter. She planted a vegetable and fruit garden and raised rabbits and chickens, both for the pot and for sale.

During this period, she also spent some months in San Francisco painting decorations for a ballroom. She raised sheepdogs for sale. She made pottery and rugs to sell, and when times became very lean, sold off part of the lot on which the house stood.

Elsewhere in the world, the war in Europe ground on for four long years; a revolution in Russia overthrew the czar; women in Canada were given the vote, grudgingly, province by province; the CBC commenced national radio broadcasts; and the first exhibition by the Group of Seven took place in Toronto. But for Emily, consumed as she was by the requirements of each day, the world had shrunk. In 1919 her sisters Edith and Clara both died. Gone were the days of travel and exploration. She painted, but her output was severely curtailed and her outings to sketch were limited to the immediate neighbourhood. She had sporadic contact with other artists who passed through Victoria, and here and there she occasionally exhibited a picture or two. But the necessity of earning money left her tired and without the spark that is essential for creativity. The artist in her did not die, but lay dormant.

Many years later she would write about her years as a landlady, dramatizing them in one of her most popular and best-loved books, *The House of All Sorts,* but for fourteen years, until 1927, Emily Carr became, as she said herself, a little old lady on the edge of nowhere.

CHAPTER FOURTEEN

A Canadian Artist

In 1927, at the age of fifty-six, Emily Carr despaired of ever realizing the vision she carried within herself. She assumed that her career as an artist was over. There had been no major works or exhibitions in over a decade. But sometimes in life it can seem as if fate is at work. Call it a conjunction of disparate events, call it serendipity or just coincidence. Nineteen twenty-seven was Emily's annus mirabilis—a miracle year. Seemingly overnight she was plucked from obscurity and placed in a national spotlight, beginning the incredible flowering that would be her greatest achievement.

This is what happened. The National Gallery of Canada in Ottawa was planning a major exhibition entitled Canadian West Coast Art: Native and Modern. Emily's work came to the attention of the gallery's director, Eric Brown, and he visited her studio, selecting paintings, rugs, and pottery for inclusion in the exhibition.

In November, Emily travelled to Ottawa for the opening. The works on display consisted of Native art and artifacts, mixed with the paintings and sculpture of such contemporary Canadian artists as A.Y. Jackson, Lawren Harris, and Edwin Holgate. A number of women artists were also included, among them Pegi Nicol, Anne Savage, and Florence Wyle. Emily had the greatest number of works, twenty-six paintings, as well as rugs and pottery. She was also asked to design the cover of the exhibition brochure, which she did, using borrowed Native motifs, and which she signed "Klee Wyck."

Her visit to Ottawa, as well as Toronto and Montreal, was a revelation. She saw for the first time the works of the Group of Seven painters, and met some of them, as well as a number of other artists. She was praised for her work, and for the first time, she found herself in the company of artists who shared her interests and, more importantly, accepted Emily as one of them.

When she looked at the paintings by Harris and others in the group, Emily saw, as she noted in her journal,

> a world shorn of fretting details, purged, purified;
> a naked soul, pure and unashamed; lovely spaces
> filled with wonderful serenity. . . . I think perhaps
> I shall find God here, the God I've longed and
> hunted for and failed to find. Always he's seemed
> nearer out in the big spaces, sometimes almost
> within reach but never quite. Perhaps in this newer,

wider, space-filled vision I shall find him . . . above
the swirl into holy places.

The transformation of Emily's fortunes might have seemed
like a sudden apotheosis but, with hindsight, we can see that
many strands in her life were slowly coming together, and the
point where they all met was where Emily happened to be
waiting. And when the strands separated again, she was one of
them, a major tributary.

Early twentieth-century Canada was a tentative enterprise, a nation in transition from colony to independence.
Many political thinkers believed in a vision of Canada as a
country united from sea to sea, incorporating not only
English Canada but also the French and the Native populations, and distinct from both Britain and the United States.

In politics, in commerce, and in culture, people looked
within their borders for national autonomy and identity.
The provinces had been gathered together under a federal
system, and a national railway helped bind them together.
But Canada's past, and its identity, were closely entwined
with those of Britain and France. Most people traced their
origin to Europe. The new Canada needed its own myths
and images, drawn from its own landscape.

Artists were part of the turning away from colonial
attitudes. Many rejected, as irrelevant to the Canadian

experience, both the English landscape tradition and the domestic imagery of French Post-Impressionism. They wanted something that was authentic to their own country—in both style and in subject—and that was also modern. But, as yet, there was neither a national art style nor a movement comparable to those in Europe.

One fact dominated the imagination of the country: the wilderness. Nature is formidable in Canada. It evokes awe and terror and an impulse to come to terms with the mystery of its vast spaces. Some painters believed they could capture the spirit of the country through landscape painting, by showing both the physical and spiritual essence of the lakes, forests, and mountains. Europe had landscapes, but none as sublime and majestic as Canada's, and none that were as yet unpainted.

In the 1920s a handful of like-minded painters in Ontario joined together and called themselves the Group of Seven. They shared an interest in painting the landscape. But not just any landscape. They wanted to paint something unique to Canada, in a style that was also unique to Canada. The position they took was radical: they would paint in a modernist style and they would paint the wilderness. Perhaps even more radical, for the times, was the idea that through direct communion with the wilderness, a truly

Canadian style and technique could arise that would be the visual definition of the nation.

In building an image of themselves, the group drew on two symbols: that of the prospector and of the trapper. Both represented straightforward, hardy outdoorsmen in the best Canadian tradition. Not for these painters the convenient studios and comfortable drawing rooms of the cities. They travelled by canoe and lived in shacks and tents as they explored the uninhabited regions of the country.

When Emily met members of the group, and saw their paintings, she was struck by how much their intentions echoed hers. She, too, had been striving to define her experience in relation to a unique, sparsely populated landscape, and to find an original style in which to paint it. She wrote in her journal of the group, "I know that they are building an art worthy of our great country, and I want to have my share, to put in a little spoke for the West, one woman holding up my end." In the beginning, the group met with derision from both public and critics, but gradually their enterprise began to succeed. They also had their supporters, notably in Eric Brown, the director of the National Gallery. Brown favoured not only the development of the group's nationalistic impulse, but also the promotion of modernist styles. However, for better or for worse, the group was based in

Ontario. Although some of its members made painting trips to the West, they could not be considered representative of the nation as a whole. This fact was not lost on Western artists, who protested their exclusion from exhibitions at the National Gallery.

A colleague of Brown's, Marius Barbeau, an ethnographer from Ottawa's Victoria Memorial Museum, had an overriding interest in the Native arts of the West Coast. Barbeau was familiar with totem poles. He saw them not only as something unique to Canada, but also as having stylistic similarities to the abstract elements in modern art. Brown and Barbeau planned the Exhibition of Canadian West Coast Art: Native and Modern together, intending to point out the similarities between the new modern painters and Native traditions. Modernist painting originated in Europe, and members of the Group of Seven were influenced by it, but by linking the Canadian version to Native art a historical precursor and inspiration could be established, suggesting a shared identity.

Both Barbeau and Brown knew of Emily Carr. As early as 1921 the Victoria painter Sophie Pemberton, who had achieved such success in London and Paris so many years before, recommended Emily's paintings to Harold Mortimer-Lamb, an arts patron from Vancouver. He in turn sent an enthusiastic letter to the director of the National Gallery. Not much came of it, but at some point Barbeau visited Emily in Vancouver and bought two of her paintings. It was he who suggested that Brown also visit her.

While the 1927 exhibition was not quite propaganda, it did have an agenda, both didactic and nationalist. Emily Carr fit that agenda as a modernist, as a Westerner, and as someone who embodied the hardy, pioneering spirit that the Group of Seven promoted as specifically Canadian. The fact that she also made use of Native motifs further recommended her to the organizers.

Most of the works Emily exhibited had been made some time before 1927, but now, as a result of the attention, she threw herself into developing her "Indian" pictures, with the added inspiration of the paintings she had seen in Toronto, especially those of Lawren Harris. The effect on her of seeing the group's work was revelatory. Her diary entries from the trip to eastern Canada are passionate and effusive. She felt that, at last, she had seen a truly Canadian art, and that there was a place in it for her own work.

Emily returned to Victoria brimming with confidence. She immediately set out on a sketching trip to the Queen Charlotte Islands, and then on another up the Skeena River, effectively recapitulating the trips she had made years earlier.

But now she went as a mature artist, not so much interested in ethnographic investigation or to make records, but as a painter returning to her source of inspiration. And although her style absorbed the influence of Harris and the group, it developed along its own original lines. The group had staked out their part of the country and now she did the same with hers. She shared some of their interests but defined herself as separate, as a woman, and as a Westerner. She wanted to paint what had not yet been painted, and through her own sensibilities.

Emily began to exhibit much more, and to achieve wider recognition. Above all, she was taken seriously as an artist at last. Success, one could call it, although sales were still few and far between.

In the following decades Emily Carr's paintings would be constantly on exhibition, not only locally, but also in Toronto, Montreal, Seattle, Amsterdam, and London. She would travel again, to eastern Canada as well as to New York and Chicago, not as a student but as an artist the equal of any other. And when she settled down once more in Victoria, the woman who had once felt so isolated and lonely would receive a constant stream of visitors—artists, students, journalists, academics, and even the merely curious who had heard about the famous painter in their midst.

Following that landmark year of 1927, her work would evolve into the distinctive style we know today. All the threads of a lifetime would come together—the landscape, the modernist palette and styles, the Indian motifs, the desire to make a Canadian art, her spirituality—all of it synthesized in paintings of intensity and power. She would also begin to write stories and biographical works. In her lifetime, she became as well known for her writing as for her painting.

Emily had always had admirers, but now, on more than one occasion, the word "genius" was linked to her name. Many people were simply astonished that they had never heard of her before. Once she had been regarded as an outcast and misfit. Now, increasingly, she was seen as someone who represented her place and time, and something much more. In 1939, when the exhibition entitled A Century of Canadian Art was mounted at the Tate Gallery in London, Emily Carr would be represented by four paintings and be described as a truly original and distinctive "Canadian" painter.

CHAPTER FIFTEEN

Lawren

Emily's most significant and fruitful encounter on her 1927 trip was her meeting with Lawren Harris, one of the founders of the Group of Seven. His was the work that most impressed her and with which she empathized most strongly. In her diary from the period she writes, "Those pictures of Lawren Harris's, how I did long to see them again . . . I have never felt anything like the power of those canvases. They seem to have called to me from some other world, sort of an answer to a great longing."

Harris invited Emily to visit him in his studio on a couple of occasions. They spent long hours in conversation. They seemed to have an immediate affinity for each other. Following these visits Emily wrote down detailed descriptions of the paintings she saw in the studio, and a few pages later, describing the view from the train, she uses the same lyrical language, as if she were seeing the landscape through Harris's eyes.

Harris completely supported the nationalist enterprise in which the Group of Seven was engaged, but it was apparent to

Emily that he also thought of art in religious and mystical terms. He told Emily that she had got the spirit of the country into her paintings, and he probably meant "spirit" in more ways than one. Harris saw the originality in Carr's approach to her subject matter. He understood the contribution she was making to the new Canadian art. He wrote to her saying, "I feel there is nothing being done like them in Canada . . . their spirit, feeling, design, handling, is different and tremendously expressive of the British Columbia Coast—its spirit perhaps far more than you realize."

Harris and his wife were very much interested in theosophy, a school of thought whose adherents saw the northern landscape as a source and expression of the divine force that animates the world. This struck a chord in Emily's always latent religiosity. She felt that Harris had succeeded in expressing a spiritual essence in his work. "Although the rest of the Group pictures charm and delight me, it is not the same spiritual uplifting," she wrote in her journal of December 1927. Harris's paintings "satisfy a hunger and rest the tired in me and make me so happy . . . they make my thoughts and life better. . . . It is as if a door had opened, a door into unknown tranquil spaces. . . . I seem to know and feel what he has to say."

Harris recommended some books to Emily, and before she left Toronto she managed to find two of the titles, one on art and the other on some of the mystical ideas in which he was interested. She read the books, thought about them, and discussed them with Harris in the correspondence that subsequently developed between them. Of these letters, Emily commented in her journal, "They were the first real exchanges of thought in regard to work I had ever experienced. They helped wonderfully." Although they were separated by age (Harris was fourteen years her junior) and by background, it is clear that the two artists had a strong friendship. In Harris, Emily had found a mentor, a teacher, and something of a soulmate. Although, in her journals, she deprecates her own work in comparison to Harris's, it is evident that she saw herself as his equal. She admitted that his work influenced her, not that she wanted to paint like him, and that he was after something she wanted, too.

Another mentor influenced Emily, the painter Mark Tobey. Almost twenty years younger than Emily, he had travelled widely, and was considered a progressive and modern painter who also had an interest in the mystical aspect of art. He made her acquaintance on visits to Victoria, and communicated some of his ideas about the formal directions painting should take. However, writing about him in her journal, Emily said, "He is clever but his work has no soul.

It's clever and beautiful. He knows perhaps more than Lawren, but how different."

Harris was not the only artist to appreciate and promote Emily's work—younger artists, like Max Maynard and Jack Shadbolt, were constantly trying to arrange exhibitions for her as far afield as New York—but Harris remained her most forceful champion. One of Emily's best-loved paintings, *The Indian Church* from 1929, was purchased from an exhibition in Toronto by Harris, and hung in his dining room. When Emily dropped Native motifs from her subject matter and began to paint only the forest, it was at the suggestion of Harris. In a letter, he advised her to "Put aside the Indian motifs, strike out for yourself, Emily, inventing, creating, clothing ideas born of this West, ideas that you feel deep rooted in your heart."

When Emily was despondent or depressed, she often expressed herself in letters to Harris, who would write back with calm, fatherly advice. "For goodness sake, don't let temporary depression, isolation, or any other feeling interfere with your work. . . . When we enter the stream of creative life, then we are on our own and have to find self-reliance." Their correspondence flourished and their friendship continued over the years, with Emily visiting Harris and his wife in Toronto and receiving visits from them in Victoria. Through Lawren and Bess, she was also introduced to a wider circle of artists and intellectuals.

After Emily passed away, Harris was one of the pallbearers at her funeral and one of the trustees of her paintings and sketches. *Growing Pains,* Emily's autobiography, is dedicated to Lawren Harris.

CHAPTER SIXTEEN

Some Ladies Prefer Indians

Around the time of the 1927 exhibition, an article on Emily Carr appeared in the Toronto *Star Weekly* with the title "Some Ladies Prefer Indians." While the article in some ways misrepresented both Carr and the Native people she had visited, it was indicative of the degree to which Emily's name was being associated with images of Native art.

But who were these Indians?

"Indian" was a word used generically to describe the original inhabitants of Canada before the European arrival. The word has been replaced in common usage by other terms: Aboriginal, Native, First Nations. The peoples that Emily Carr encountered on her travels comprised the Salishan, Nootka, Kwakiutl, Nisga'a, Nuxalk, Heiltsuk, Haida, Tsimshian, and Tlingit. All of these tribes were linked, either through trade and shared customs or through language.

From the first encounter between European and Native, the relationship was contentious and fraught with difficulties and misunderstandings. As European settlers spread throughout British Columbia, the Native communities suffered disruptions and stresses that altered their way of life. Traditional trade and hunting and fishing practices were curtailed or superseded by the cash economy in the form of logging enterprises and the many canning factories that employed Natives. Native land was appropriated, and legislation was enacted to hinder Native land claims. At the same time, various government bodies banned certain ceremonies, like the potlatch, all with the intent of assimilating Natives into the wider economy and community. Many of the villages that Carr visited were abandoned, either because they were inhabited seasonally, or because the population had been decimated by diseases such as smallpox and measles. Sometimes entire communities were relocated by the government when their land was appropriated.

The general view was that the First Nations were a vanishing race whose art and culture were doomed. The cause of their imminent destruction—the presence of the new settlers—was not acknowledged. The European settlers dismissed Native art and culture as part of a primitive, prehistoric past, and as incompatible with that of the new arrivals. Carr was no stranger to First Nations people. The Songhees reserve was just across the harbour from her home when she was growing up. During her early years, there were almost as many Natives as whites in Victoria. Native women would sell game, berries, or handicrafts from door to door, and were sometimes employed by white families as domestic help.

The general attitude toward the Natives around Victoria was patronizing at best, frankly racist at worst. Natives were seen as a general nuisance, as an urban blight so close to the city, and as a constant source of trouble. The Songhees reserve would eventually be moved away from the city, as the land became desirable to Victoria's newer citizens. Christian missionaries were the first Europeans to establish a presence in coastal settlements. Their proselytizing mission was to bring Natives into the Christian community. Native art and customs were denigrated as heathen and primitive, and their world view was discredited and dismissed. With time, churches and schools were established in Native communities, and then further afield. Eventually, many Native children were sent to reside in schools that banned their languages.

In early 1899 Emily was invited to visit the Presbyterian mission school at Ucluelet. The mission had been established five years previously as part of the effort to convert the Nootka people to Christianity. Already, at this point in her life, Emily had little patience for the missionary project. Although she came to Ucluelet as a tourist and a spectator, she made a genuine effort to get to know some of the inhabitants. It was here that she was named Klee Wyck, the laughing one, from her humour-filled efforts to communicate across the language and cultural divide. She was impressed by what she saw as a dignified people, at home in their coastal forest landscape. She saw that there were other ways to live than the one she knew in Victoria. As the child of immigrants, aware of her own culture's recent arrival in North America, she might even have envied the inhabitants of Ucluelet for their sense of belonging. Emily had recently returned from three years of study in San Francisco and thought of herself as an artist. She took watercolours and drawing materials with her, and sketched the inhabitants of the village as well as their houses and canoes. There were no totem poles or decorated house fronts of the kind she would paint elsewhere, but this first contact made a profound impression upon her. It was not until her trip to Alaska in 1907 that Emily encountered totem poles and began to form her ambitious project, to travel to as many Native communities as possible and to make a pictorial record of the totem poles. She was aware of the enormous transformations

Native culture was being subjected to by white society, and this may have been why she undertook what she saw as a socially meaningful project.

Before Marius Barbeau became aware of Emily's paintings, he had encouraged and assisted other artists to visit and paint in the Upper Skeena River region. In an early example of corporate sponsorship of the arts, Barbeau secured free passage for the artists from the Canadian National Railway, which had extended its line to the area. In return, the railway company received commercially exploitable images with which to promote tourism. Carr would later participate in the same venture. A brochure from the CNR used one of her paintings in an advertisement that encouraged readers to

> Visit the land of the mystic TOTEM. Romance, tradition, the history of an age-old people are carved on the totems of British Columbia. Grotesque, heroic, they tell of war and peace; life and death; singing a veritable saga to those who can read them. In quaint native coastal villages they await your spellbound gaze.

The various artists' paintings that resulted from Barbeau's venture present the Native villages as picturesque sites, and show no understanding of either the inhabitants who had lived there for hundreds of years or of the totem poles that belonged to them. A comparison between these other paintings and Carr's representations of the same sites shows that she strove for more than a merely scenic view.

Barbeau and Brown's attempts to include Native art in a national cultural identity did not necessarily mean that the Natives wanted to be included. They were not consulted. The arrival of tourists in the villages on the railway was sometimes seen by the local inhabitants as a further extension of colonization.

One of the artists from Ontario who visited the Skeena in 1926, Edwin Holgate, went on to decorate the tea room in the Chateau Laurier Hotel in Ottawa, which was owned by the Canadian National Railway. The tea room and adjacent dance hall were done in the "Skeena River Style." It is unlikely that any Natives took tea there. Similarly, no Natives were invited to the opening of the Canadian West Coast Art: Native and Modern exhibition. The Native works in that exhibition were drawn from museums and private collections and presented as art, with little attention to the function of the items shown or to the context in which they were created.

Modern critics have condemned non-Native society for using Native art inappropriately. Some have challenged the popular views of Emily Carr's association with Native peoples. On many counts she is guilty as charged. She did sometimes exploit her Native connection in the establishment of her own artistic identity. She made rugs and pottery for sale that used Native designs, and she allowed them to be included in the National Gallery exhibition. She also designed the cover for the exhibition brochure with Native motifs and signed it Klee Wyck, thereby enhancing her identification as an individual with privileged knowledge of Native culture. She neither learned any Native language nor had extensive contact with Native peoples, except on her painting trips. In her later writings, she demeaned Native society to humorous ends. But if she sometimes acquiesced in the romantic notion of Natives as noble savages, her writings show that she also saw them as people like any other, possessing the same virtues and faults.

Emily Carr was very much a part of her time, and embodied many of the prevailing attitudes that patronized the Natives. In her defence we can say that no other artist, and very few people at all, took as much of an interest in Native culture as she did. She hardly benefited financially from this association, and always had misgivings about using their motifs in her art. Her depictions of the totem poles are accurate; while being artistic interpretations, they neither intentionally distort nor misrepresent what she saw.

West Coast Native culture had neither a written language nor a pictorial tradition outside of carving and decorating. The paintings of Emily Carr have given us a record in pictures of objects that have been dispersed, destroyed, or have simply disappeared.

It is important, even crucial, when looking at her paintings, to be aware that what we see are, first of all, images of Emily Carr's relationship to the totem poles she saw. She was an artist, and it is the right of the artist to paint whatever she chooses. They are only paintings, after all; however we may use or interpret them, they remain the expression of one person's imagination. They are not a pronouncement, a definition, or a decree. In fact, her paintings of totem poles can even be seen as a homage of sorts to Native art.

In the totem poles, Emily saw something that had been lost or obscured in European art. It was stark, bold, larger than life, and hinted at the magical and supernatural. They were a fusion of art and what Emily would term religion. The poles have a profound relationship to the environment in which they were developed. Emily responded to an extremely powerful human expression made by people living close to the source of life. Native art was the doorway that led her to that source and helped her become an artist of distinction. She never lost sight of her inspiration's origin, and always acknowledged her debt.

CHAPTER SEVENTEEN

Sophie

In many of the photographs of Emily's studio, a small portrait of a woman is visible on the wall. The painting is a watercolour made by Emily in 1914. The subject is Sophie Frank.

Emily's account of their meeting is told in *Klee Wyck*, in the chapter titled Sophie. In 1906 Emily went to live in Vancouver. One day a woman selling baskets, accompanied by her three children, appeared at Emily's door. Emily wanted one of the baskets but did not have the money to pay for it. Sophie agreed to accept some clothes instead, and returned later to collect them. She lived on the Salish reserve in North Vancouver, across the inlet from the city. Soon after, Emily visited her on the reserve. So began a friendship that would last thirty years.

Close friendship between Natives and whites was unusual. A kind of apartheid existed that kept the two groups apart physically and socially. The relationship between Emily and Sophie took place within unequal spheres of power and entitlement, but it prospered nevertheless. Sophie's situation was a difficult one. Most of her children would die in childbirth or infancy, and both she and her husband sometimes succumbed to alcoholism. Sophie and Emily did not mingle in society at large—their visits were always private. Usually it was Emily who visited the reserve. As a white woman, she had easier access to the Native community than Sophie would have had to a tea room in Vancouver.

Emily wrote about Sophie in *Klee Wyck* in a tone that, to the modern ear, is patronizing and overly picturesque. Curiously, she mentions in the story that Sophie's English was good, yet the words she gives to her are in pidgin English. Nevertheless, the two women were friends. Sophie even named one of her children after Emily, although the baby lived for only three months. Many of Sophie's other children also died at young ages, and there were fifteen family graves in the cemetery to which she took Emily on one occasion.

Sophie was an artist, too, and the designs she used in her baskets inspired Emily. Sophie also served as an interpreter of Native culture to Emily, opening many doors. The two women visited the Catholic mission church next to Sophie's house and exchanged letters often. When they met, Emily talked of art and her travels; Sophie told her stories from the world of the First Nations. In Sophie's calm, stoical acceptance of a diminished life, Emily found an example of strength and balance to carry her through her own travails. In *Hundreds and Thousands,* Emily wrote of Sophie, "Her love for me is real and mine for her. Somewhere we meet. Where? Out in the spaces? There is a bond between us where colour, creed, environment don't count. The woman in us meets on common ground and we love each other."

Although Emily came to be identified in popular imagination with Native peoples, Sophie was really her only true, personal contact with a Native person. After Emily left Vancouver and moved back to Victoria, the two women maintained a correspondence, augmented by Emily's visits to the mainland.

In a letter in 1929, Sophie wrote:

> We feel sorry you was sick with the flu and I hope you will be strong in the near future. . . . Yes, I am selling baskets and making baskets for my living. Frank can't work now. He got odd jobs once in a while. Well, my father is old now and his house got burned a month ago. I feel bad for I cannot get to go and see him up Squamish Valley. . . .
>
> Your friend,
> Sophie Frank

The letters to Emily were almost always signed "your dear friend," or "your ever loving friend."

Sophie remains a vague figure in the life of Emily Carr. We know little of her other than the details recounted in Emily's writings and the evidence of a few remaining letters. Sophie's family history, her stature in her own community, how her baskets were regarded by her own people—all of this is left to conjecture. Sophie's lapses into alcoholism and prostitution were not uncommon among her peers, and the societal causes were many: racism, poverty, inadequate health care, segregation. For all these reasons, Sophie remains largely unknown to us and her voice is silent.

Sophie and her husband, Jimmy Frank, must have given Emily many insights into Native culture. Emily's knowledge of Native art could not have come only from printed sources or her sporadic contact with people in the villages. Certainly, the lecture that Emily gave in Vancouver on the context of her paintings of totem poles must have been informed by Sophie's contributions. In December 1939, Emily received the following letter:

My dear friend,

I guess you thought I forgot you but I still think of you. So I just thought I would drop a line and let you know how I'm getting along. I am quite well at present as I still staying at Squamish as I left North Vancouver after my wife died.

I'm keeping away from drink. I'm better off here. I'm having a hard time but I get along.

I cannot forget my wife. It's pretty hard and sure is very lonesome without her. I hope you are well and please answer.

Jimmy Frank

Klee Wyck, Emily's first book, was dedicated to Sophie Frank. She died five years before it was published.

CHAPTER EIGHTEEN

Animals

In practically every photograph that exists of Emily, from childhood until her last years, she is in the company of animals. This is one of the most singular aspects of her personality: she simply could not live without the companionship of a pet of some kind. At different times in her life (and sometimes in combination and in multiples) she had a cat, a duck, a hen, a rooster, a horse, a crow, a peacock, a thrush, a blackbird, a bullfinch, a vulture, a cockatoo, a parrot, a chipmunk, a squirrel, a raccoon, a white rat, a rabbit, and dogs, dogs, dogs. (She owned dogs as pets, and also raised and sold more than three hundred of them in a commercial venture.) And most famously of all, she had a monkey.

Even when she travelled she took at least one animal with her. On her trip to France, when the boat stopped at Liverpool, she went to London, purchased a parrot at a bird market, and took it with her to Paris. Earlier, when she was ill in England and confined to a sanatorium for months, she managed to collect some nests of baby thrushes and finches, which she raised in her room. She planned to take these songbirds back to Victoria with her, and let them populate the woods with their singing.

On her painting trips, when she went to the northern forests, a dog always accompanied her. Cougars and bears inhabited the forests, and there were semi-feral dogs and cats near the Native villages. Emily's own dogs served not only as companions on her solitary excursions, but also as sentinels and guardians.

A portrait of Billy, her sheepdog, completed in 1909 and rendered with great sensitivity and skill, shows that Emily could have had a career as an animal painter. But, except for two paintings of the monkey, Woo, made when Emily was in her sixties, and a few early watercolours of parrots, there are no other paintings of animals in her entire output. The fact that she did not paint her countless pets is curious. But then, she didn't paint people much either.

Depictions of friends and family, creatures and pets, are reserved for the other side of Emily's creative output: the comical drawings and her writings. Emily might at times have been melancholy, or irritable, but she had a tremendous sense of humour. We see this in her cartoons, where she lampoons not only those around her, but also herself. Her paintings have a gravitas to them, but the cartoons and verses show the other side of her personality. The same might be said of the photographs. Usually they show a rather sober woman, but when the photographs capture an unposed moment, she is often smiling and laughing. Her smile is often either mischievous or radiates great warmth. And, after all, hadn't she once been called Klee Wyck, the laughing one?

There is a popular misconception that Emily wandered the streets of Victoria in bohemian garb, with her monkey perched on her shoulder. It is an image that has been promulgated in films, children's books, and biographical sketches, and it has contributed to the picture of her as an eccentric. The image is colourful, but erroneous. At home, the monkey often scampered loose, and Emily dressed as she pleased, but she always had a strong sense of propriety. When she went out she always dressed appropriately, in a manner befitting a middle-aged matron from an established family.

But what of the monkey? Who was Woo?

Around 1923, when she was in her early fifties, Emily saw a Javanese monkey caged in a pet shop. She rescued the creature by purchasing it. Emily named the monkey Woo, after the sound it made, and this little creature would be her constant companion for the next thirteen of its fifteen years, until they were separated by old age.

Emily made only two paintings of Woo. One dates from the early 1930s and shows Woo standing upright, holding onto a branch with her hands. She is wearing a yellow pinafore that has an enormous bow on the back. The face, shown in profile, is remarkably human.

Emily did dress her monkey in a pinafore on occasion, especially during the wet cold months. Java is a tropical country, and Emily was concerned for Woo's health. No doubt when Woo was dressed up, the temptation to see this lively, affectionate, mischievous creature as a kind of little girl would have been irresistible. And, perhaps Emily also saw a part of herself in Woo: that independent little girl who was once known as Small.

There is another painting of Woo, done much later, perhaps one of the last pictures Emily did. The first Woo is made to seem human, but in the later painting she stares back at the viewer, defiant and wild. No sweet little girl in this creature. Against a background of swirling branches and green fruit, an untamed animal looks out at us with blazing yellow eyes. This is a creature from the other world, that we glimpse only rarely, where Emily trod more often than most of us ever will. Perhaps this is a self-portrait, showing her dark and moody side.

We can only speculate about the need these animals filled. The most obvious conjecture is that they took the place of the children Emily never had. Perhaps Emily might have found in the company of animals the unconditional love that was either difficult or lacking in her contact with humans. These animals were her friends. She could hug, fuss, nurse, and mother them at will.

Anyone who has lived with pets knows that they seem incapable of malice, betrayal, egotism, or cruelty. Dogs, especially, seem to desire only to love us and enjoy our company. They possess an essential simplicity that is close to a state of grace and without the tragedy of human self-consciousness. They live within their limitations, whereas humans constantly chafe against theirs. There is a holiness and an innocence in animals that would have appealed to Emily's religious nature. Perhaps contact with animals was also a way of being in touch with that same element she perceived in the forests— the non-human aspect of nature.

CHAPTER NINETEEN

The Face in the Mirror

If a painting is a mirror of the artist, whose is that face looking back at us?

There are no films of Emily Carr. There are black-and-white photographs. There are caricatures drawn by her own hand. There are descriptions by friends and acquaintances. There are a couple of painted self-portraits, and her own writings. So, what did she look like?

In a photograph of the five Carr sisters, taken in 1888 when Emily was seventeen, it is easy to distinguish Emily from the others, for she was physically unlike them. The Carr women are slim, narrow-faced, and their expressions in the photograph are amiable. Emily's face is more oval, the eyebrows more arched, the eyes more almond-shaped. There is only the slightest resemblance to her mother. In the photograph, Emily is the pretty one. Her expression is guarded and watchful.

She was described as a dreamy and sensitive child, but also as mischievous and independent. A photo of her at sixteen shows a wistful girl with a pet crow on her lap. In England, a friend described her as sturdy, with a mass of dark curly hair. A photo from this period shows a much more serious young woman of thirty-one, without that youthful, pensive, dreamy look.

She always had a sense of humour. In the caricatures from her time in England, she lampoons herself wearing a cape and tam-o'-shanter as she paints in the woods. When she returned from England she had gained weight, no doubt as a result of the forced inactivity and the experimental diets at the sanatorium. Self-caricatures of her in France show a rather stout woman buttoned up in coat and hat, with an umbrella tucked under her arm. It is true that she never dressed to be attractive and had little regard for what others thought of her appearance. Her clothes were simple and mostly black. She didn't wear makeup and was scrupulously clean. In later life, she almost always wore a black knitted cap or a black headband to restrain her hair.

Her friend Edythe Hembroff-Schleicher described Emily in 1930 as a round, solid little person, with a wrinkle-free face and merry, blue-grey slanted eyes. Her voice was soft and melodious, with something of an English accent. In the photos taken of her as an adult she is often smiling, her eyes twinkling, and one can imagine the radiance of that smile.

Emily had a reputation for being difficult to get along with, yet she always had many friends, and was known by them to be generous and affectionate. She sometimes accused others of selfishness and egotism, but had her fair share of those traits. She had always been an outsider: within her own family and as a colonial in England, a foreigner in France, a Westerner in Toronto, a white among Indians, and an artist among those who had no understanding of her art. She was also separate from the mainstream of society and other women, because she was without a husband and children. Any of this was enough to make her sensitive to slights and criticism. Her journals show that she often felt lonely, neglected, and depressed.

In her diary, on the last day of 1940, at the age of sixty-nine, Emily wrote: "To paint a self-portrait should teach one something about oneself. I shall try." She also wrote, "I hate painting portraits . . . pulling into visibility what every soul has as much right to keep private." Carr was intensely private in many ways, preferring to project her feelings into painting and writing. She was also prudish about her body, self-conscious about her weight, and never thought of herself as a suitable subject for a painting. There are very few known self-portraits of Emily.

One of the first, from 1905, when she was about thirty-four, depicts Emily and her dog, done in charcoal and pastel. The two faces, both with curly hair and expressive eyes, are painted with facility and present an accurate likeness. The picture is conventional, although she obviously felt that both she and the dog were out of the ordinary, judging by the title, *The Rum'un and the Oddity*.

Another self-portrait was painted in 1925, when Emily was fifty-four, and is much more unusual. The artist is seen from the back, her face invisible. One hand holds a palette and brushes, the other is raised to the easel. The red straps of an apron are visible around her neck. It reminds me of a painting by another independent and maligned woman who suffered prejudice because of her choice of career—the early seventeenth-century painter Artemisia Gentileschi. Her *Self-Portrait as the Allegory of Painting* was made in Rome three hundred years before Emily's painting, yet the pictures are astonishingly similar. Emily might even have seen the earlier painting in London, where it is part of the Royal collection. Although Artemisia's face is visible in a three-quarter view, she too holds a palette and brushes in her left hand while her right hand is raised to the canvas. She too wears a green dress. Instead of an apron string around her neck, she wears a gold chain to which a little masklike face is attached. Even the face of Artemisia, with its rounded cheeks and black hair, puts us in mind of Emily.

In a standard self-portrait, the artist looks forward in a frontal view, using a mirror to capture the pose. A more complicated arrangement of mirrors would have been necessary for both Emily and Artemisia to see themselves in the unusual perspective they chose, and no doubt the pose is intentional, for the pictures lack the quality either of vanity or self-scrutiny associated with a mirror. Both women want to be acknowledged as artists, not only by painting their own portrait, but also by showing themselves in the act of creating the picture we are looking at.

A late self-portrait by Emily dates from 1938, when she was sixty-seven years old. It was done on paper with thinned paint, and is dashed off with all the bravura of an artist in complete command of her brush. She looks out at the viewer directly now, almost glares, almost a force of nature herself. The portrait is solid and uncompromising. The colours are all earth and forest tones. The brush strokes swirl and swoop. Flecks of white highlight the nose, a corner of the mouth, an errant wisp of hair. The mouth is set, still determined. The eyes are full of intelligence. The picture is grand and stately, and has the same frank self-acknowledgment that we see in Rembrandt's magnificent late self-portraits. Here I am, the painting says, confronting us: a woman, a human being. It is an extraordinary painting.

There is another way for an artist to make a self-portrait, and that is to imbue some inanimate object with qualities she sees in herself. The term used for this is anthropomorphism: to endow non-human objects with human feelings, thoughts, and sensations. Human qualities can also be attributed to animals, representations of deities, and natural phenomena. The anthropomorphic tendency is often found in religion, mythology, children's stories, and of course in art and literature.

Emily found such a representation in a totem pole. She called the figure Zunoqua, the wild woman of the woods, and she met this woman three times. The meetings are described in her journals and in the story "D'Sonoqua" in the book *Klee Wyck*.

The most striking of the paintings that resulted from these meetings, and one of the most unusual in the whole of Carr's work, is *Zunoqua of the Cat Village*. Filling the left side of the picture is a stylized figure with exaggerated dark eyes and a grimacing mouth. The head is draped with a serpent. Behind the figure, the vegetation is a whirl of swirling green waves, from which the faces of yellow-eyed cats stare out. The effect is uncanny. The words that Emily used in her journal to describe her experience are forceful and evocative: "ferocious, creepy, full of unseen things . . . that was some place! There was power behind it."

In *Klee Wyck,* Emily describes how she arrived in a remote village with only an Indian girl as a guide. In the drizzle and mist, on a rocky bluff, she stumbles on the path and looks up from a bed of nettles to see a creature looming above her. "She seemed to be part of the tree itself, as if she had grown there at its heart." The eyes bore into Emily and she imagines that the life of the cedar is looking out and the voice of the tree is coming from the mouth of the carved figure. Years later, Emily comes upon a similar figure, and this time her descriptions are similar to those used by others to describe Emily herself. "The whole figure expressed power, weight, domination, rather than ferocity." When Emily asks who the figure represents, she is told that it is the wild woman of the woods.

On the third occasion when she meets the figure, Emily sees it as a young and fresh singing spirit, graciously feminine and womanly. The wild woman is now shy and untouchable. It was while she was painting this figure that a swarm of feral cats came out of the forest and surrounded Emily, a dozen of them, purring and rubbing her ankles, one even jumping into her lap.

We can speculate that Emily saw herself in the carved poles she painted, as one of those silent, isolated figures, alone, noble, and proud. In light of her written descriptions, we can look at the painting of Zunoqua as not sinister at all, but as an image of integration. The animals, the art, the forest, and the woman are all one together—a self-portrait of the spirit.

CHAPTER TWENTY

The Painter

Musing about art in her journal, Emily jotted down this thought:

> I do not think that most artists could tell what
> was their aim in art exactly. It just grew and
> grew from a small beginning. It necessitates
> much digging and searching, burrowing as deep
> as one is able and the using of our hearts as well
> as our eyes.

One can become a painter by learning the requisite skills and techniques, but to become an artist is a different matter entirely. Emily wanted to make something that was true and real. She could not see what she wanted to make, but her intuition and her desire told her that it existed—if she could find it. She felt blind and alone because what she wanted to make had never yet been seen. She wanted to make something entirely new. The task seemed almost impossible, but she went forth, into the unknown.

All children like to draw, and then, as they grow older, they abandon the pastime. But with a little encouragement, some persist. Emily was one of these. The Carr family had never produced an artist of any sort. Emily was the first. She had some natural talent and some ability, but above all, she had the desire.

When Emily was eight years old she drew a picture of her father's dog, using a bit of charcoal from the fireplace and a scrap of paper. Years later, after her father's death, it was found among his papers. On the back he had made the notation, "By Emily. Aged 8."

She also drew a couple of family portraits from a photograph. When her father gave her some gold coins and commissioned her to make copies of the portraits, she set up a studio in the pantry. She was further encouraged when drawing lessons were arranged.

She wanted to learn more. She sought out teachers, first in San Francisco, then in London, and once again in France. She also learned a great deal from two other artists, Mark Tobey and Lawren Harris. But her greatest lessons came in the forest, from studying totem poles made by carvers whose names she never knew.

No artist emerges from a vacuum or works in one. The idea of the solitary genius is a myth—a myth sometimes encouraged by the artist herself. Emily Carr was not some untutored creator simply expressing herself in paint. She studied her art and was exposed to many influences. The fact that she absorbed and transformed those influences into something unique is a testament to her ability. The kinds of paintings Emily made are a result of deliberate choice and intention. Earlier works of hers show that, if she had been so inclined, she was quite capable of painting conventionally realistic landscapes, portraits, and still lifes. She certainly could have made a career painting that way.

In France, Emily was exposed not only to technical changes, but also to new attitudes that allowed her to think of her subject matter in a new way. Painters like Van Gogh and Gauguin, and later, others like Picasso and Matisse, were interested in what was called the "primitive" in art. They had turned away from the nineteenth-century academic tradition of realistic painting to seek out what they believed was a more authentic subject matter. This took the form not only of painting directly in the landscape, but also of seeking out peasant subjects. This can be seen in some of the paintings made by Gauguin and Van Gogh in Brittany, for example, in which the folk customs and costumes of the French peasantry are much in evidence. Gauguin would later go to Tahiti in search of something untainted by European ways. Picasso and others would look to African masks and sculpture. These forms of non-European art were seen as fresh and original and as a source of renewal for an art that had become stale and decadent. All of this was part of a Romantic search for renewal and a return to something authentic, to a purer form of art in areas that had not been absorbed into Western industrial culture. This tendency certainly validated Emily's interest in Native art, and gave her the confidence to pursue it when she returned to Victoria.

By her own account, she came back from France with a "new way of seeing," a better understanding of colour, and a way to use it expressively. When she returned to the forest and looked at the totem poles, the way they stood out against the greens of the trees would have been stunning. She would have noted the bright colours, the black outlines on the forms, the stylized way of representing figures and animals. In Native art, she saw colours that were not tied to an actual description of an animal or figure. Later, when she went deeper into the forest, the works became more sombre, the hues those of leaf and branch, but there is a tremendous variety in the greens, and all sorts of colours are used, subtly and with great refinement.

Through the eyes of someone educated in European art, the totem poles and decorated houses would have seemed unusually colourful and stylized. The innovative way in which animals were transformed and incorporated into the design would have appeared novel and striking. At the same time, this was a living art, not something meant to be displayed in a gallery or museum. The totem poles were integrated into their environment. They were of the place and the people.

Emily wanted to be a Canadian painter. Even when she was in England she talked of wanting to paint the landscape of British Columbia rather than the pretty English countryside. After her first meeting with the Group of Seven painters she wrote in her diary: "Canada and her sons cry out for a hearing but the people are blind and deaf. Their souls are dead. Dominated by dead England and English traditions while living things clamour to be fed."

She could have stayed in Brittany. Concarneau, where she studied, was a popular artists' colony, and many painters settled there. There were even Canadian painters who had left for France, never to return, who developed a French style. But Emily was of a different place. The light and the colour of Brittany were not for her. Even though she retained what she had learned about colour, she eventually abandoned the bright Fauve style for the moist greens and the dark shadows of the forest. One of the fathers of Impressionism, the landscape painter Corot, who worked in the forest of Fontainebleau outside Paris, had advised younger artists to "seek the muse in the forest." Emily might have read that advice, for she followed it, literally, although the muse she sought came in a form that would have astonished Corot.

Native art gave her an entry, a stepping stone. Like the Native people, she had been born in this place and grown up in it, albeit in different circumstances and with a different perspective. Nevertheless, she was of the place, and she knew it in her own way.

On her trips to Toronto, she had seen the freshness in works by the Group of Seven and been impressed by their depiction of the country, but she was of the West Coast. That was her land, and that was what she wanted to paint.

In strictly stylistic terms, the greatest influences upon Emily were Mark Tobey and Lawren Harris. Tobey visited Victoria a number of times and boarded with Emily. He also gave a master class for local artists in Emily's studio. Tobey was very interested in the formal aspects of a painting; that is, how a painting is composed, where the lights and darks are placed, how a shape can be simplified or abstracted. Harris, too, had simplified his depictions of the landscape. In his pictures, mountains, trees, and water are stripped down to basic forms that are bathed in a soft, raking sidelight. Both Tobey and Harris would eventually develop a purely abstract painting. The general trend in painting during the first six decades of the twentieth century was toward simplification, culminating in pure abstraction. The belief that abstraction could better depict or create in the viewer a spiritual state was just as important as any more formal experimentation.

Carr's pictures from 1928 onward use many of the devices that Tobey and Harris employed. The totem poles become iconic forms. The trees and foliage in the forest are like sculpted wave forms. The light now seems not so much to fall on objects as to emanate from them.

Emily began to redesign and structure the forms of the forest in her paintings. This is the work of someone who is not copying what she sees, but is thinking about what is in front of her and then synthesizing it into something novel. She paints pictures of the totem poles, but she does not copy them, nor does she adopt the stylistic devices of the Native artist. The style of the paintings is her own. It is the feeling that these objects create in her that is of interest to the artist she has become. Eventually, she goes to the source from which the totems originate: the spirit of the place. The power that she feels emanating from the forest begins to emanate from her own work. While there is always an awareness of the formal devices in a painting, her later paintings are intensely emotional as well.

Emily did not take an intellectual approach to art, but she was by no means ignorant of modern trends. She had many books with titles such as *How to See Modern Art, The New Art, Painters of the Modern Mind,* and *Western Art and the New Era.* Many of the passages in these books were underlined and annotated by her.

During the 1920s she was often visited in Victoria by artists from Seattle and Vancouver. As well as her trips to Toronto, where she met with Harris and others, she visited New York and Chicago and made the rounds of the galleries there. She met Georgia O'Keeffe, another innovative woman painter who drew her inspiration from nature. Emily was also given a private tour of a collection of avant-garde paintings by Katherine Drier, an author and connoisseur. How much of what she saw directly influenced her is debatable. Carr, like most artists, was concerned with the task at hand. If an idea was useful to her own immediate concerns, she noted it. If not, then it had no effect. Both the ruminations of critics and the judgment of history were irrelevant to her.

Her career as a painter falls into a rough sequence of styles. First were the landscapes done in the English tradition, and then the documentary studies of Native motifs. With her return from France, a new vigour in the brush strokes and a brightness of colour are evident. After the meetings with Harris and the Group of Seven, there is a simplification of form and a stronger emotional content. The paintings become dramatic and symbolic. Finally, in her late style, she comes out of the forest into the sky: the paintings are full of movement and energy.

How is a painting made? Well, you find something you want to paint. It might be a tree, or an apple, or your own face. You use a pencil to make a drawing. Very difficult, even if it is just an apple you are trying to draw. Then you take some colour and apply it. But what colour? How much? How to mix that particular tone? How to blend the brush strokes? What to do about the background? Very difficult.

But how to actually make a painting? Most of Emily's oil paintings were based on sketches that she made directly in the landscape. She would begin with a pencil drawing. No doubt she had a little tray of watercolours and a pad that she could hold on her lap. Once the drawing was done, she applied the colours. The paint dried as quickly as the water evaporated. First impressions and sensations were what counted at this stage. These sketches might have taken just a few minutes, or much longer if close observation was important, as it was when she wanted to get the exact details of a totem pole. She was always scrupulous about that. In the paintings made before 1927 she always strove for accuracy and exactness, with the idea in mind that she was making a record for history.

Later, in the studio, she used these little watercolours as the basis for her big oil paintings. During the winter months she would cut pieces of lumber, mitre the corners, and assemble a frame on which a piece of canvas would be stretched. She then applied a ground of white paint to the canvas to seal it and provide a smooth surface. Once this had dried, she could begin working up one of the summer sketches onto the canvas. She would make a simple outline with a brush dipped in thinned paint. Sometimes she changed the composition from the one in the sketch, because reality doesn't always arrange itself into a pleasing layout. When she was satisfied with the composition, she would begin to block in the basic shapes with colour.

She preferred to work in privacy—a thoughtless comment from an onlooker could ruin her concentration and sow doubt. Often she would sit and look at a canvas for long hours without lifting the brush. She wanted the painting to speak to her, to reveal what it was becoming. She did the same thing when she was in the landscape itself, sitting and looking, listening to her inner voice and the voice of the forest. Sometimes she failed to hear what she was listening for, and gave up. But she always came back; she always persevered.

A close-up view of one of her paintings reveals that the way she used paint was not in the least bit naïve or accidental. In some parts the paint is thin; in others, thicker patches are placed to catch the light or emphasize a texture. Colours are very subtly placed next to each other, as when a violet or orange appears in the midst of a swath of green. In some sections the colour is intense and pure, then it becomes restrained and suggestive. The abstraction of the forms, the selection of viewpoint and focus—all are refined and deliberate. Like a violinist drawing all the nuances out of the strings, from the most forceful march to the most delicate pizzicato, she used her brush as a delicate instrument, not only as a tool but also as an extension of her very self.

Often, as they get older, artists develop a more fluid, almost impatient style, with a very loose brush stroke. One sees it in the last works of Rembrandt, Titian, and Picasso. They are aware of their failing health and fading eyesight. At this stage, an artist has achieved perfect technical mastery. The movement of the painter's hand becomes quick. Attention is directed toward achieving the big effect, going straight to the heart of the matter. Detail is either subordinated or ignored.

There is no time for equivocation. At the very end of her career, Emily switched to using paper instead of canvas as the support, and cheaper paints thinned to a liquid consistency with turpentine, and on occasion, gasoline. Contrary to the myths about Carr, she did not do this out of poverty, but in order to be able to work out of doors on a large scale in oil paint. An oil painting usually takes days, or even weeks, to dry, but thinned and applied to paper, the paint would have some of the same properties as watercolour in its liquidity and drying time.

If there is one artist she can be compared to at this stage, it is Van Gogh. In both his last paintings and hers, subject and method are united. All the shapes and forms become flowing brush strokes that display a tremendous intensity. Carr sometimes seemed rough-hewn and crude, but her technical ability was the equal of any painter's, and she surpasses most of her peers in her sophisticated understanding and employment of the visual language of painting.

The mature works upon which Emily's reputation rests were the result of long years of development. The paintings we now look at, and can recognize as Emily Carr's, came about after much struggle, through the meeting between what she learned in France and what she saw in the totem poles. The mature painter neither copies nor represents her subject. It doesn't matter if she is an innovator or an original; what matters is that she makes something true. But there is never a finished style in an artist's work. There is always evolution. There is always the next painting to be done.

Whatever her influences were, she transcended them. As a painter, her goal finally was not to make a picture of a subject, but to make a work of art that stood alone. The subject of the painting is the painting itself. It is from that rectangle of coloured pigment that all meaning and beauty must flow. Carr brings the painting out from the forest, and what we see, what we perceive, is not a picture, but a sensation. The painting is pure sensation, which we in turn experience. Emily Carr, the painter, immersed herself totally in her own experience and created something that is partly the forest, partly herself, but mostly something else entirely.

· In her best paintings, Emily Carr is no longer describing the forest or landscape, but painting an equivalent of the experience of being in the place. The paintings are masterpieces of construction: they are imaginative, they are interpretations, they are facts. And that is what makes them so marvellous and admirable. Sometimes, when I look at her paintings, I can only shake my head in wonder and admiration.

CHAPTER TWENTY-ONE

The Loves of Emily

The relationship with the first man in a woman's life, her father, can lay the pattern for what follows in her relations with all men. Richard Carr was fifty-three when Emily was born. As the youngest girl, Emily was her father's favourite. In the morning, when her father walked to his business, Emily accompanied him as far as the bridge. She was there again to greet him when he returned in the afternoon. They shared a love of flowers and birds. He once remarked that she should have been the boy in the family.

Something happened between them when she was in her teens and, after that, she was no longer his favourite, and he was no longer hers. She referred to it as the "brutal telling," and only in her last years was she able to write about what had happened. Evidently, Richard Carr, rather than his wife or the older girls, explained the facts of sex and reproduction to Emily. She described it as horrible sex things told disgustingly. The effect was traumatic and devastating, and she remembered it vividly in an unpublished journal written when she was in her sixties:

> Telling me things a happy innocent child should not hear and telling them in a low and blatant manner. I couldn't forgive Father, I just couldn't, for spoiling all the loveliness of life with that bestial brutalness of an explanation, filling me with horror instead of gently explaining the glorious beauty of reproduction, the holiness of it.

Richard Carr died a few years later, when Emily was seventeen. His death left the matter forever unresolved. In later years, when she read Richard Carr's own diaries, she saw him as strong, brave, honest, and kindly. But at his funeral she stood over his grave looking down into the hole, and felt relief. Her mother had died two years earlier and she was now without parental authority and structure. The early death of parents always leaves a scar, and in some cases, the wound underneath is never healed.

When Emily was twenty-eight years old she fell in love with one man, and a different man fell in love with her. She would break the heart of one, and the other would break hers. She was not ignorant of what goes on between men and women. She had lived on her own at art school in San Francisco. She was aware of the facts of sex, not only from her father, but also from seeing animals mate. Her sister Clara had married and had children of her own. Nevertheless, Emily was a naïve and inexperienced young woman, and for her, a kiss was more than just a kiss.

The identity of her first love is unknown. He took her into his arms and kissed her at a garden party. We have to assume that is all that happened. But the effect was overwhelming. First love is not only emotional, it is powerfully physical. Yet the love Emily felt for this man was not returned, and she said that it took her fifteen years to kill the feeling. Her own words speak eloquently of her pain. They were written in 1935, when she was sixty-four, and although they seem to refer to this incident, the passionate intensity with which she writes can lead one to speculate that there might have been another great love in her life:

> And the love of the lover sweeping you clean off your feet, making you forget the horrible sex things told so disgustingly when you were a little child, things that frightened you horribly. And yet in the passionate love of the lover, forgetting every bit of the horror, willing to give every bit of your body and life and love in floodtide ocean fairly drowning the beloved, and to find it was not

wanted and never, never, to quite know why, only
to know it must be so, and to eat one's heart out
alone always, never daring to tell a soul, shamed
and broken and hurt at your own indecency, of
loving so furiously, so overwhelmingly—unasked
and unwanted—to find the caresses and kisses
were only sport, selfish amusement, your heart
used as a shuttlecock, batted furiously hither and
thither only lasting one game, thrown aside, feath-
ers broken, balance broken, a hideous, battered,
smashed-up toy that could never be mended or
straightened again. Only good for one game, then
finding its way to the garbage can, grimed and
fouled. Oh love, poor love. Not mended or
soothed and strengthened but murdered and
thrown out and towed far far out to sea and
dumped. Oh!

That passage stands out in all of literature as one of the great
cries of anguish from a wounded woman's heart.

And then there was the other man, Mayo Paddon.
Emily met him on the steamer trip to Ucluelet, up the
west coast of Vancouver Island in 1898, when she was
twenty-six. Paddon was the purser on the ship. In one of
those curious synchronicities that life throws up, this was

also Emily's first significant encounter with First Nations art and life. Paddon and Emily became friendly. He called on her often in Victoria. The young couple could even be said to be courting. Paddon proposed. Emily demurred. For some time, Emily had been planning to continue her art studies in England. That year she left for London. While she was there, Paddon appeared. He proposed daily. She refused daily. She did not love him. Besides, she had just embarked on the beginning of a long-held ambition—to become a real artist. She knew all the benefits that marriage would bestow on her: stability, a place in society, a home, and children. But she had also seen her own mother subservient to Richard Carr. Emily said that her mother was always Mrs. Father, never Mrs. Mother. As for children, Mrs. Carr had been worn down by nine pregnancies, and died at the age of fifty.

The difference between being a mother and an artist had been demonstrated dramatically to Emily some years before. In San Francisco she had boarded in the house of a woman artist, who was also a widow with small children. The woman struggled in poverty and could not afford proper medical care when one of her children became ill. Emily wrote of the incident, "Art I hate you, I hate you! You steal from babies!" Art demands a price from the artist, and in that incident, Emily had a glimpse of the reckoning. She knew that marriage would stifle her art.

Paddon stayed for three months in London before he finally accepted her refusal as irrevocable. He burned all the letters they had exchanged, and later married someone else, but for years afterwards, Emily received a pressed flower from him every Christmas.

Love for Emily would never again be erotic. Two other men were significant in her affections: the artist Lawren Harris and the broadcaster Ira Dilworth. While both men were younger than Emily, they functioned as older brothers, Harris as an artistic and spiritual mentor and Dilworth as her literary adviser and editor.

Emily used the word "love" frequently in her reminiscences and correspondence. In two other cases, referring to a woman and a girl, she meant the word more than casually.

Around 1922 she became friends with a twelve-year-old pupil boarding at Alice's school. Her name was Carol Williams. They shared a love of animals and had a similar sense of humour. Carol wanted to be an artist, and Emily gave her painting lessons. They began to see one another daily. Carol helped her dig clay from the cliffs for the pottery-making enterprise Emily had started. She probably boarded with Emily while at school—her parents lived forty miles away—and even went on a brief sketching trip with Emily. Emily called her "Baboo," because she said she had always wanted both a baboon and a daughter. Carol called Emily "Mom." So close did they become that Emily asked Mrs. Williams if she could adopt Carol. Mrs. Williams declined the offer.

In the companionship of this little girl, Emily found not only an outlet for the maternal love she contained, but also a way of being a child again. It was one of the happiest periods of her life. In 1926 Carol moved to Ontario, and later married. They remained close for the rest of Emily's life. In the last photograph of Emily, taken in the summer of 1944, shortly before her death, she is sitting in a wheelchair on the cliffs in Beacon Hill Park. The woman standing next to the frail but smiling Emily, one hand resting on Emily's shoulder, is Carol.

Emily tended to befriend the underdog, the waif, the excluded. And if she did not actively campaign to change her friends' situation, she certainly empathized with them. She might have been guilty of condescension, and she seems never to have questioned the automatic entitlement she enjoyed, but in these ways she was very much a product of her times. This is not to diminish her warm heart.

Over the years, it has often been said that Emily sublimated all her erotic impulses into her paintings. Commentators have found phallic imagery in the tree trunks, and womblike associations in the cavities and hollows of the forests. It is worth remembering that the theories of Sigmund Freud, which are usually evoked in these interpretations, are speculations, more literary than scientific, and might say more about the viewer than about Emily Carr. She herself was offended when she heard about such interpretations. Like Georgia O'Keeffe, who was subjected to the same speculations and vehemently resisted them, she knew that if she acknowledged that line of interpretation she would become notorious and diminished as an artist. Her paintings celebrated the fecundity of natural life, but they were always about many other things as well.

She assumed a maternal role in many of her relationships. She acknowledged that, unless someone has been a parent, that person could not know the true fullness of life. When it came to marriage and parenting, she felt herself to be incapable of "the life-long building up and tying down to another's will, not being free." That was the reckoning she paid for being an artist. Some of her maternal feelings were bestowed upon her art, as she wrote in her diary:

> I feel about my paintings exactly as if they were my children. They are my children, of my body, my mind, my innermost being. When people call

them horrible and hideous I resent it deeply. I can't help it. I know people don't have to like my pictures, but when they condemn them I feel like a mother protecting her young.

Emily has also been characterized as a social misfit, a kind of hermit, possessing too prickly a personality to form relationships with other people. Far from it. She probably had a wider and more inclusive social life than most other people, men and women, of her time.

Perhaps because she was a single woman, dependent upon the social support of other women, Emily maintained friendships with a great many people throughout her life. Whenever she travelled, whether it was in Europe or eastern Canada, or to remote villages in British Columbia, there was always someone, some family connection or acquaintance, upon whom she could call for hospitality. She must have been likeable to have made so many friends.

It was her sisters, finally, whom Emily loved best and longest. They were her most constant friends and companions. They always lived within walking distance of one another and saw each other almost daily. Although the relationships had all the tensions that can exist between siblings, and were often contentious, the sisters were life-long companions.

In the end Emily became like a nun in her love, which became spiritual, a love turned outward and away from the personal, toward what she called God, that divine presence which she found in the forests.

CHAPTER TWENTY-TWO

Her Little Book

Most Canadians first heard the name Emily Carr on the radio, and it was not because of her paintings, but because some of her stories were being read aloud over the air. In fact, as her fame spread across Canada, many people did not even know that she was a painter. They thought of her as a writer, author of the bestselling *Klee Wyck*.

Emily had always been something of a secret writer. As a young woman she had written poems and kept a diary, which she stored in a green cloth bag, and forgot for many years until she unearthed them when she was in her mid-sixties.

During the 1920s, when she wasn't painting much, she began to write little sketches and anecdotes surreptitiously, not showing them to anyone, mindful of the disdain with which her paintings were often greeted by family and acquaintances. In 1929 she enrolled in a correspondence course with her friend Flora Burns. In the evenings the two women would compare assignments and give critiques of each other's work. Soon, Emily bought a second-hand typewriter and learned to use it. Her spelling and punctuation left much to be desired, and Flora took on the task of correcting Emily's writing.

Later, she sent some of her stories to Lawren Harris and other friends, and the response was encouraging. Harris even suggested she write an autobiography. She had resumed writing a journal in 1927, but for the moment she was content to stick with something less ambitious than a full account of her life. The stories she wrote instead were usually about her encounters with Native culture and about her childhood.

In 1934 she took a summer course in writing, and then another one that winter, and began to submit her stories to various magazines, including *Maclean's* and *Saturday Evening Post*. The rejection slips piled up, but she wasn't deterred: she had lived a life of rejection. She persevered. She tried sending her manuscripts to publishers, but these were also rejected. One was even lost.

She studied writing as thoroughly as she had studied painting. She took courses and sought advice. And when she had absorbed what she considered useful, she turned her back on her critics and teachers and went her own way. One of those teachers, Ruth Humphrey, to whom Emily gave a painting in return for instruction, would prove to be instrumental in boosting her writing career.

In 1937, at the age of sixty-six, Emily suffered a heart attack. During her recuperation, unable to paint, she completed seventeen stories in six months, while lying on her back and writing with a pencil in her notebooks. Ruth Humphrey showed Emily's stories to Ira Dilworth, the regional director for the Canadian Broadcasting Corporation. Dilworth was familiar with Emily, having grown up in Victoria, and he was immediately impressed by the originality and freshness of the writing. He arranged for some of the stories to be read in a nationally broadcast radio program in 1940, doing the reading himself. And he went further, submitting the manuscript to Oxford University Press in Toronto. The collected stories about Emily's travels in British Columbia and her exploration of Native culture were published under the title *Klee Wyck*. Dilworth took over the job of editing Emily's writing, and during the process, with Dilworth correcting the manuscript's spelling and grammar while sitting across the table from Emily, a great affection sprang up between them. Like Lawren Harris before him, Dilworth became a mentor and friend.

Dilworth was thirty years younger than Emily. He had been a teacher before he took a post with the Canadian Broadcasting Corporation. He lived in Vancouver with his ailing mother but made frequent trips to Victoria to work with Emily on her manuscripts. The letters between them are tender, full of affection, and constitute a literary gem in their own right. Emily made a pun of Dilworth's first initial and addressed him in her letters as "Eye," and often signed off with "Your loving Emily & Small."

When he first read her stories, Dilworth wrote to Emily that he was lifted from his "stupid humdrum existence into something exquisite and beautiful."

When Emily gave her affection, she gave it unstintingly. More than two hundred letters to Dilworth exist. In 1942 she wrote to him, saying:

> The love I gave you certainly was not the type I gave to my sweetheart, a love that expects a whole heap back. It was a better love than any of these; its foundation was in lovely things. . . . Perhaps the kind of meaning my love has for you and I'd like yours to have for me is comrade; comradeship seems so expansive somehow, a turning into things together.

In her last years, Ira's affection was crucial to Emily. She had never really loved a man, but toward Dilworth she expressed all the love that she contained. A few months before she died in 1944, she wrote to him, "I've been so proud of your friendship, and my love for you has been very deep and sincere. I can't imagine life since I had to give up painting without it." Dilworth reciprocated the affection in his own letters to Emily, writing that, "You will never know how much your confidence and love have meant to me." His letters were signed with "bundles of love."

Emily's reminiscences of her childhood, published as *The Book of Small,* is dedicated to Dilworth, and in her will she made him her literary executor, as well as leaving to him the royalties from her books. The foreword to *Growing Pains,* Emily's autobiography, closes with these tender words by Dilworth: "High in the Canadian sky wild geese, great flocks of them, are shouting their mysterious cry. They are all going on as you and I must, Emily. Life will not stand still. So, fare forward, dear soul."

When *Klee Wyck* was published, readers were captivated by the adventures of this solitary woman in an exotic environment, and it was an instant success. For many, this was their first glimpse into the British Columbia landscape and the world of the West Coast Native peoples. While we now see some of Emily's attitudes toward that world as outdated, her accounts were generally considered to be sympathetic.

Klee Wyck received the Governor General's Literary Award for Non-fiction the year after it was published, and has remained a classic of Canadian literature ever since. *The Book of Small* followed in 1942. Emily resurrected her childhood nickname, Small, and lets that character enact the remembered incidents from her youngest years. In her final years she wrote little, but there were manuscripts waiting for a publisher. Shortly before her death, in 1944, a recounting of her years managing a boarding house was published as *The House of All Sorts*. In it, Emily tells of the ups and downs of that period, with its odd characters and odder happenings. *Growing Pains,* the official autobiography of Emily Carr, the artist, appeared a year after her death.

Two other books were published in the 1950s, and then, finally, her journals from 1927 to 1941 were published in 1966. The collected works, published together in an omnibus edition, run to almost nine hundred pages, a considerable achievement for a woman who published her first book when she was sixty-nine years old and who was incapacitated by two heart attacks and two strokes. She was a force of nature to the end.

In her writing, Emily found a way to express the intimate, private side of her personality. She was never interested in painting the personal details of her life, but always sought a larger quality that was more universal. Other than the journals, which were not written for publication, all her books are fiction of sorts. They were written from the perspective of a woman approaching seventy years of age, so what she recalls is, first of all, not immediate, and second, is structured and altered with the intention of making a good story. That the stories are vivid and original in the telling is a testament to her talent as an author.

The autobiography *Growing Pains* must also be read as a selective account of her life. Much is omitted, sometimes intentionally, and much is misremembered. Emily, after all, was always aware of her reputation, and had a hand in crafting her own myth. But, as subsequent biographies have demonstrated, the essential story of her life is authentic. In *Growing Pains,* and in the other books about her life, she is often self-critical, and the book served her as a self-examination and as an assessment of her life.

From the moment she became publicly known, a constructed figure called "Emily Carr" began to emerge. This figure is partly factual and partly invented, by Emily and by others. Emily knew that if she didn't craft her own image, she would inevitably be misrepresented. She wanted to be self-created. Her relations with journalists and critics were conflicted. She resented their intrusions, but wanted their attention, and wanted to be taken seriously. She also knew that art criticism is a kind of vivisection, destroying what it attempts to explain. Her publications are an attempt to control her own biography—to name herself.

Her humour is evident in all her writing. She sometimes mocked others, but she never excluded herself as an object of ridicule. The caricatures she drew when she was young, and the satirical verses she wrote to accompany them, were especially sharp.

For the modern reader, her style, values, and attitudes can seem archaic. She sometimes exemplified the prejudices and racism of her times. She often portrayed the Natives as simplistic. Nevertheless, her books remain readable and are without malice.

The book that offers the most candid insights into both the woman and the painter is her journal, *Hundreds and Thousands,* named after a small, multicoloured candy from England that Richard Carr poured into the Carr children's hands from a big jar—to their great delight. Emily called the journal "my dear little book," but it is so much more than that. It stands as one of the great records of an artist's thoughts, rivalled only by the letters of Vincent van Gogh or the diaries of the painter Eugène Delacroix. Here is a soul laid bare, confessing to her doubts and aspirations, turning to the book both in moments of joy and in moments of black despair. Sometimes the book is a prosaic record of daily life, and as such, it is a fascinating account of a specific time and place. Sometimes it is a confessional, where everything that is left out of the fiction appears in candid detail. She tells us about her struggle to realize a painting, and about the technical details of how it is made. There are animals, family, neighbours, and tenants. Sometimes it is heartbreaking to read, and sometimes it is pure poetry. Above all, the book is the naked voice of one woman, but one who speaks for the human heart in all of us.

The last lines in that journal, written on March 7, 1941, three years before her death, end with the words "carry on, carry on, carry on."

CHAPTER TWENTY-THREE

Into the Mystic

An inclination to mysticism is not a Canadian trait. It is tolerated in poetry, less so in painting, but is usually regarded with embarrassment at best, or seen as unhealthy at worst.

Canadians prefer to regard themselves as sensible, sober, and down-to-earth, not given to excess in matters of belief. "Reason over Passion," as Pierre Trudeau might have put it. When it comes to religion, Canadians have a preference for the innocuous United Church's mild Presbyterianism over any of the more demonstrative forms of worship. Religion asks and answers the big questions: Who are we? Where do we come from? Where are we going? It also provides a code of moral and societal behaviour, answering the question: How shall we live? The religious impulse has never been entirely dormant in human culture. Some thinkers have proposed that it is the primary force at work in human consciousness—the drive to find and understand our place in the universe. Its expression is often powerfully manifested in the arts.

The Church, in whatever denomination, prefers to be the mediator and explicator of all things spiritual, and looks with suspicion on individual paths to wisdom. It tends to be intolerant of paths that lead beyond its theology. It prefers to be the authority that dispenses and interprets dogma and iconography and tends to frown upon religious expression in the arts when it falls outside the canon.

Emily grew up in a conventional Christian household, set in a Christian society that took its cues from the Anglican Church. Everybody was religious; churchgoing was an act that confirmed your place in society, and while you needn't worship with fervour, it was expected that you believed in the Church.

The Carr household wasn't fanatically pious, but on Sundays Emily's father insisted upon prayers, Bible readings, and Sunday school classes organized by one of the sisters. Sunday was not a day for leisure or idle entertainment. Emily's sister Lizzie was interested in doing missionary work among the Indians, a vocation to which many young women of the era aspired as a way of being useful, since so many other occupations were closed to them.

Emily, from an early age, resented the way religion intruded on her life, and she found her sisters too prim and orthodox. She also felt that a certain amount of hypocrisy lay behind their conformist demeanour. After the break with her father, she considered his religious expression fraudulent. Her experience at art school in San Francisco was liberating: Without the dictates of parental authority, she no longer participated in her sisters' prayer meetings or Bible study groups, or felt compelled to attend church services.

Her later encounters with Native art showed her that there were other ways to express the religious impulse. Aside from their practical functions, the totem poles presented a cosmology different from the Christian one. Christianity had no place in this world of rain and forest and people whose stories made no mention of Jesus.

In Carr's lifetime, the identity that Canadians promoted to themselves and the world was a virile, masculine one. The arts, or any concern with the heart and the emotions, were seen as soft, self-indulgent, too feminine, and fundamentally unserious. The Group of Seven painters were promoted as pioneers at work in the forests—hardy trappers and hunters who just happened to paint well. Their art was seen as fresh, with none of that soft decadence that characterized the old European art. And if their painting looked to some viewers a bit like the dangerous modernism infecting the arts, the growing consensus was that this was an art made sharp by the bracing winds of Georgian Bay and the hard sunlit colours of Algonquin Park in the fall.

Painting, of course, was part of culture, which was generally preferred in a form that had been approved already in Europe, was easy to understand, and somehow contributed to moulding a healthy and uplifting character. True, art could also harbour sensualists, bohemians, misfits, and modernists who had no respect for tradition and who preferred the primitive to the civilized. But they were best ignored or dismissed.

This image of the hardy, no-nonsense Canadian art is still widely believed in today. However, the new style of modernist painting, of which the Group of Seven was a regional manifestation, had for a long time had an undercurrent of interest in spiritual pursuits. The sources were many: English Romantic poetry, German anti-materialist idealism, the symbolist movement, the ideas of the American transcendentalists such as Ralph Waldo Emerson, Henry David Thoreau, and Walt Whitman. And, of course, theosophy, a movement that had a profound effect on Canadian art.

A strong mystical tendency existed in the Group of Seven, but this was de-emphasized or obscured by the nationalist program. They used terms such as "the spirit of the landscape" freely, but there was little analysis of exactly what that spirit was. Even today, nature is seen as a place for healthy exercise, such as hiking, or as a place to think about ecology. Awe, terror, and rapture are not mentioned.

Theosophy was not a religion, a philosophy, a cult, or a church. The Theosophical Society was founded in New York in 1875 by a Russian, Helena Blavatsky. After she had travelled in various countries, she developed what could best be described as a synthesis of religious and mystical thinking in order to arrive at a way of understanding the divine and achieving spiritual wisdom. By the 1880s the Society had become an international organization with branches in India, across Europe, and in Canada and the United States. It drew on Buddhism and Hinduism, traditional Western religions, and on more esoteric traditions. Independent religions were something of a phenomenon in the late 1800s, and many of them were of the most dubious kind. Theosophy, too, had some precepts that verged on hocus-pocus, but then, so do the established religions.

As it affected Emily, theosophy is relevant only because of Lawren Harris, and the way he translated some of its suggestions into his art and encouraged her to do the same. The essence of what Emily took from Harris and theosophy can be summed up in the idea that through contact with nature we can experience the animating principle that governs the universe. The artist can articulate that principle.

For a time, Carr tried to adapt her thinking to the principles of theosophy, but eventually rejected it, not without feeling some guilt that she was betraying Harris.

Yet she longed for connection, and for a way to express that connection, for a way to find a new god, or the old gods. She rejected orthodox Christianity and theosophy, needing no doctrine, or finding none that corresponded to her own experience. In the totem poles, Emily saw a total expression of Native cosmology. It came out of their society, which was part of the landscape and the forest. Emily saw it as art that expressed the West Coast landscape. If we see a Greek sculpture, we might not know which god or hero it represents, but we can still respond to the sculptor's depiction of a human being. In the same way, Emily responded to a depiction not of a culture, of which she remained somewhat ignorant, but to the way that culture expressed itself. Through it, she could discover and articulate what she had only felt before.

The forest can be mysterious, sinister, inhospitable, and unknown. It occupies a powerful place in our consciousness, hovering there with a primal intensity. In Emily's day there was no poetry, no painting, no music, and no literature through which to approach this unknown. The anonymous carvers of the totem poles led Emily toward the shadows, and in them, she found a way to the light. "The power that

I felt was not in the thing itself," she noted in her journal, "but in some tremendous force behind it."

In the 1930s Emily began to attend church again, as well as all sorts of lectures dealing with spirituality. She even invited one speaker home and showed him her paintings. Her thoughts were directed very much to expressing her religious feelings in her painting. In her journals from this period, the word "God" is repeated a great many times, and always linked with nature. When she talks of God she uses the language of Christianity, but it was a god that was a result of a personal approach. As she stated in her private notebook, "God in all. Always looking for the face of God, always listening for the voice of God in Nature. Nature is God revealing himself, expressing his wonders and his love. Nature clothed in God's beauty of holiness." Emily herself said that churchgoers might have thought of her as outside the Church, and she preferred to visit empty churches, but she was religious and always had been. The forest became her church. In some paintings, the trunks of the trees are reminiscent of the pillars inside a cathedral, and the shafts of light are like those that fall through the windows of a church.

Painting from nature became a form of meditation and prayer, a way of communing with and being part of the divine spirit that is the universe. The act of painting had itself become an act of worship. In her journal, Emily described her method of approaching nature:

> Sit quietly and silently acknowledge your divinity and oneness with the creator of all things. Enter the silence and feel yourself pivoting on the one source and Substance God. When you are permeated with this feeling of oneness with the creator regard that which is before you till some particular phase of it arrests your attention and then form your Ideal, thinking deeply into it, seeing God in all, drawing the holiness of his Idea to you and absorbing it till you become one with it, and at home with your subject. Rely on your intuition, which is the voice of God to lead you and tell you step by step how to proceed. The working will come through the Spirit.

In nature she saw the underlying life force that is in everything. Her paintings communicate that same intensity, mystery, and awe she had experienced when looking at the totem poles or sitting in the woods. She painted not as an observer, but from the inside—inside the forest and inside herself. Whatever mystical notions she projected onto the landscape, they were not mere romanticism, for she was aware of the biological forces at work in nature, and saw them as evidence of the pulsing life that is in everything. "Though everything was so still, you were aware of tremendous forces of growth pounding through the clearing, aware of sap gushing in every leave, of push, push, push, the bursting of buds; the creeping of vines. Everything expanding every minute."

She infuses her work with the intensity of her religious feelings. There are no habitations, no animals, no humans in the paintings now, just nature, pure, essential, almost abstract. It was life, but outside the human context.

All her life she had sought the god spirit—to find it, to show it, and to be in it. Some painters work for praise and riches. And some work for something that most of us are unaware of until the artist brings it to our attention. Like the great religious painters of the past, she painted neither for fame nor glory, but for God.

Her spiritual yearnings found a form of expression in her paintings. Art and religion coincided. Art was the act and the symbol of the spiritual meaning she had found. The painting was not only the means but also the expression, a visual manifestation. Her final paintings have an ecstatic rapture to them that is almost unrivalled in art.

Emily's mystical quest develops in a complex, circuitous path. She begins with youthful churchgoing, and then the Native encounter, followed by Harris and theosophy, a return to the Church, a journey deeper into the forest where she paints in a new way, and then the final synthesis of it all into ecstatic rapture.

Two of Emily's most frequently reproduced paintings can serve as an illustration of her mystical development. They are *Indian Church* (1929) and *Scorned as Timber, Beloved of the Sky* (1935). In the first, a simplified white church is dwarfed by the looming sculptural forms of the surrounding forest. There is something a little sentimental and obvious in it, and yet it speaks to so many people as an image, not only of a habitation in the vastness of nature, but also of the human in the universal.

In the second painting, completed just six years later, a tall, thin tree trunk shoots up from a strip of land at the bottom of the picture into a sky of radiating light. The emotional and symbolic content affects us in an almost physical manner. The power of the painting is undeniable. It is beyond design and decoration; no longer a depiction of something that is meant to represent rapture, it is rapture, the very embodiment and expression of ecstatic liberation.

A note to herself in her diary serves as eloquent advice on how we might also approach her paintings:

> A picture is not a collection of portrayed objects nor is it a certain effect of light and shade nor is it a souvenir of a place nor a sentimental reminder, nor is it a show of colour nor a magnificence of form, nor yet is it anything seeable or sayable. It is a glimpse of God interpreted by the soul.

CHAPTER TWENTY-FOUR

The Failure and Success of Emily Carr

Is it better to have a happy life than to achieve great things? Would Emily Carr have been happier if she had chosen another path? There was never any doubt in most people's minds that Emily Carr was a genuine and original artist. Whether her work was accepted or not, it was recognized as the real thing. It was her tragedy and her gift to be compelled to make art.

Success and failure are both relative. A poet once stated that there was no success like failure, and failure was no success at all. Emily would have understood the paradox in that statement, and the irony. She was a woman of many contradictions. Her life can be seen as a series of apparent failures, yet each failure also contained within it the elements of success. She was a success because she was a failure.

When, after five years of study in England, she returned to Canada without having established herself as an artist and without having developed a personal style, she thought of herself as a failure. Yet her experience as a colonial in the motherland, alienated by a culture in which she could find no part, deepened her identification with the West Coast and gave her a stronger sense of belonging.

After Emily returned from France, her exhibition of paintings in the new style met with little success. Rather than give up and resume an acceptable way of painting, she determined to develop and adapt that new style to the landscape she knew.

If we measure a woman's success in life—as her society did—by her prosperous husband, her enviable house, her talented and beautiful children, and her elevated status in the hierarchy of society, then Emily Carr was a failure. But the choices she made also gave her the freedom to live and think independently.

The attempt to make a historical record of totem poles failed when the provincial government rejected her project and declined to fund it. Yet now we look to her paintings of totem poles as one of the few records that do exist. Furthermore, she eventually rejected the role of ethnographer and discovered something much more important in Native art—a religious identification with nature.

The lack of sales and acclaim for most of her career made her realize that fame and fortune are not the point of making art. And her isolation from the mainstream of art forced her to rely on her own inner convictions and to develop an originality that was earned and that places her above her peers in both achievement and artistic integrity.

At the end, her body failed her, with illness and old age. But by then she had achieved a serenity and a mystical sense of transcendence beyond the physical. And, finally, through the legacy of the paintings she left to the world, she achieved immortality.

The greatest success in life is how we engage with the world, how we live. It can be said of Emily Carr that she embraced life with desire, courage, determination, and passion. And that is the best kind of success.

CHAPTER TWENTY-FIVE

Epitaph

There is a story often told that goes something like this:

The heroine leaves home for unknown regions in search of a special goal or object. After many setbacks and difficult encounters, and with the aid of benevolent helpers at crucial moments along the way, she reaches her destination and finds what she is seeking. But, in doing so, she discovers the true meaning of the quest, which was not a place or an object, but an inner goal.

Most of the world's cultures have in their mythology some version of this quest narrative, whether it is in Homer's *Odyssey* from ancient Greece, medieval knights in their search for the Holy Grail, or a story as contemporary as *The Wizard of Oz* or *The Lord of the Rings*. The quest stories are essentially tales of personal transformation and can be interpreted as a metaphor for an individual's journey through life. The ultimate goal is not success or achievement, but the getting of wisdom.

The journey is always a long and arduous one, sometimes lasting a lifetime. Travel to distant and unknown places is always involved. Opponents and situations arise to block the path and challenge the heroine. There are dangers and setbacks. Sometimes the quest is abandoned temporarily when the heroine gives up and retreats. Sacrifice is always involved and courage is essential.

Emily Carr's life reads as one of these quest stories. The naïve young girl leaves home with only one ambition, to be an artist, but she does not yet understand the true meaning of art. She completes one task, to study in San Francisco, but finds it is not enough, and sets off again, this time for England. There she encounters prejudice, loneliness, and isolation. She must also sacrifice the hope of love. A setback comes in the form of illness that temporarily ends her quest. Once recovered, she journeys to France, and finds success when she develops a new painting style and has two of her pictures shown at the Salon. But the success brings no immediate benefit. The goal has not yet been achieved.

Then the journey takes her into the deep forest, where she encounters a world that is different and mysterious. She begins to develop as an artist, yet the world turns away from what she offers. She gives up the fight, having sacrificed personal happiness and her youth for an unattainable goal. The years of retreat follow.

The benevolent helper appears in the form of Lawren Harris. Like the wizards of old, he gives her the key, by indicating where the path might lie. Once more, she journeys into the forest. She thinks she has found her goal at last, in the totem pole paintings, which now bring her recognition and acceptance. But the totem poles are only signposts. She goes beyond them, into the true mystery, and it is there, in her spiritual transformation, that the journey reaches its conclusion.

At the end, Emily has become a wizard herself, and her magic—in the form of paintings and books—spreads outward to touch lives everywhere. The apotheosis comes only after her death, when she is elevated into a kind a myth herself, and what was a solitary journey by one woman becomes a story for all.

Emily Carr's grave is under the trees in Victoria's Ross Bay cemetery, on a sloping piece of land overlooking the waters she travelled so often. Her body lies there under a plain headstone, a part of Canada.

She once wrote these words in her journal:

> Dear Mother Earth! I think I have always specially
> belonged to you. I have loved from babyhood to
> roll upon you, to lie with my face pressed right
> down on to you in my sorrows. I love the look of

you and the smell of you and the feel of you. When I die I should like to be in you uncoffined, unshrouded, the petals of flowers against my flesh and you covering me up.

The marker on her grave gives no hint of the courage, the innovation, the talent, and the passion of an extraordinary person. It is a simple, small slab of stone. On it, her epitaph is engraved, modest, and to the point.

Emily Carr
Artist and Author
Lover of Nature

Somewhere, across the waters, in the deep green shadows of the forest, the totem poles and the giant trees still stand, and the spirit of a great artist still hovers around them.

1871	Emily Carr is born December 13, in Victoria, British Columbia.
1886	Her mother, also called Emily, dies.
1888	Her father, Richard Carr, dies.
1890–93	She attends the California School of Design in San Francisco.
1893–88	She teaches art to children in Victoria.
1899	She visits Ucluelet for the first time and acquires the name Klee Wyck.
1899	She attends the Westminster School of Art in London, England.
1900	She rejects an offer of marriage from Mayo Paddon.
1903	She stays at East Anglia Sanatorium for eighteen months after a nervous breakdown.
1904	Back in Victoria, she contributes political sketches to *The Week*.
1906	She takes on students in her studio in Vancouver. She meets Sophie Frank.

1907   On a trip to Alaska she sees totem poles for the first time.

1908   She embarks on sketching trips in British Columbia.

1910   She studies in France.

1912   Her French paintings are exhibited in her studio. She goes on a six-week sketching trip in northern British Columbia.

1913   Her "Indian" paintings are exhibited in her studio.

1913   She builds a boarding house in Victoria.

1914–
EARLY 1920S   She manages the boarding house in Victoria.

1924   After a hiatus, she resumes painting, and exhibits her work in Seattle. She establishes a professional friendship with Mark Tobey.

1927   She exhibits in Ottawa and meets Lawren Harris and other members of the Group of Seven.

1928   She goes on a major sketching trip in British Columbia.

1929	She exhibits frequently and goes on a sketching trip on the west coast of Vancouver Island.
1930	She travels to Toronto, Ottawa, and New York, and makes her last trip to Native sites.
1932	She travels to Toronto and Chicago, and sketches in the British Columbia interior.
1937	She has her first heart attack, and starts writing seriously for the first time.
1939	She has a serious heart attack, and meets Ira Dilworth.
1941	*Klee Wyck* is published and wins the Governor General's Literary Award for Non-fiction.
1942	*The Book of Small* is published. She goes on her last sketching trip. A major exhibition of her work is held at the Art Gallery of Toronto.
1944	*The House of All Sorts* is published. She suffers a stroke, and writes her autobiography, *Growing Pains.*
1945	Emily dies in Victoria on March 2.

SOURCES

All the statements attributed to Emily Carr are taken from her own writings.

Blanchard, Paula. *The Life of Emily Carr.* Vancouver: Douglas and McIntyre, 1987. A richly detailed and extensive account of Carr's life.

Crean, Susan. *The Laughing One: A Journey to Emily Carr.* Toronto: HarperFlamingo, 2001. An imaginative and creative approach that combines fiction and history in its examination of many aspects of Emily Carr's life.

Moray, Gerta. *Unsettling Encounters: First Nations Imagery in the Art of Emily Carr.* Vancouver: UBC Press, 2006. The most thorough and extensive examination of Carr's encounters with Native peoples.

Shadbolt, Doris. *Emily Carr.* Vancouver: Douglas and McIntyre, 1990. The best analysis of Carr's paintings.

Tippett, Maria. *Emily Carr: A Biography.* Toronto: Penguin Books, 1985. A fine and sympathetic portrait of Emily Carr.